MW01077597

FINDING THE WAY

FINDING THE WAY

By

Cindy Burkart Maynard

CINDY BURKART MAYNARD

All rights reserved.

This book or parts thereof may not be reproduced in any form,
stored in any retrieval system, or transmitted in any form by any
means – electronic, mechanical, photocopy, or otherwise – without
prior written permission of the author or publisher, except as provided
by United States of America copyright law.

Copyright pending

Author's Note

In 2017 I walked the Camino de Santiago, a 500-mile pilgrimage route across northern Spain. In 2017 over 200,000 people walked the Camino. I was impressed by that number until I learned that in 1250 AD an equal number walked the Way. I wondered what it would it have been like to walk this path in 1250?

It was thrilling for me to think that I was walking in the footsteps of Charlemagne, El Cid, St. Francis of Assisi, Lorenzo de Medici, many kings, queens, saints, and millions of pilgrims of every description who have walked this route. The alure of the Camino has inspired modern luminaries as well. More recent pilgrims include German chancellor, Angela Merkel, Anthony Quinn, Shirley Maclaine, Martin Sheen and Paulo Coelho. The spirit of these, people and the thousands of nameless pilgrims accompanied me.

After a year of research and reading I set pen to paper, well actually I sat down at my computer. Finding the Way is my answer to that question.

Contents

PREFACE

In preparation for walking the Camino de Santiago, I studied history and cultures of the various people who live along the route. The Camino begins in the Pyrenees along the border between present-day France and Spain. But before France or Spain or any of the other European countries existed this area was occupied by the Basque people.

The Basques have occupied much the same area of northern Spain and southern France for thousands of years, as attested by the archeological record. The inhabitants of this area speak a language that is not related to any other living language.

The ancestors of the Basques have likely occupied this area since the end of the last ice age 10,000 years ago or more, perhaps as early as colonization of Europe by Homo sapiens. This would make them the oldest continuously surviving people inhabiting any location in Europe.

It is believed that they have lived in or near their present location for at least four thousand years, staunchly resisting invaders and preserving their traditional culture. They were the last people in Europe to be Christianized, holding fast to their ancient culture and traditions until the tidal wave of Christianity overwhelmed them.

As a lover of history, The Basque people tantalized my imagination. This book is my effort to weave together the two cultures into the story of one girl, caught between the "Old Ways" and the onslaught of Christianity.

PART ONE

CHAPTER ONE

1250 AD

SUMMER

The animals penned in the windward half of our stone hut woke us first. The aged goat, well beyond any useful purpose, staggered to her feet, chuffing and pawing the ground. The rooster squawked and pecked at the hens to wake them up, scurrying around them until they formed a tight ball. The dog roused himself from a sound sleep. His sentinel ears pivoted forward, standing alert, his low grumble escalated into a high whine like that of a frightened child.

"Mother." Amika jostled the shoulder of the woman sleeping next to her on the straw pallet on the floor of the hut. "Listen!"

Esmene, now as fully alert as the dog, raked her fingers through her angry black locks. In a single, fluid movement, she bolted upright and reached for her hoe. Gripping it with both hands, like a soldier's pike, she held it across her chest, resolutely facing the door.

"What's happening?" Amika began. Then she heard it—the crackling of fire brands, and the muffled drumming of stomping feet.

"Go!" Esmene barked. "Grab your cloak and go. Run to the cross marking the path into the mountains. I'll meet you there."

"But Mother," Amika protested. Esmene's answer was to push the girl out the door.

Hickory bark torches, bound at intervals with thick twine, tinged the darkness with an ominous glow. More than a dozen grim-faced neighbors marched toward the hut. Leading the pack, the tall, thin Father Ricardo, and the barrel shaped Venena Arrosa were silhouetted against the smoky glow.

1

When Amika recognized the two of them leading the rowdy crowd she knew her mother was right. There would be trouble.

Without another moment's hesitation, Amika crouched and scuffled out the door and, hugging the shadowy stones of the hut, hurried to the safety of the nearby trees. There she found the familiar stone cross marking the mountain track that marched into the sleeping hills. She dashed to the stalwart beech where village and forest merged. The tree was like an old friend, its branches both playground and refuge since she was old enough to clamber into its gnarled arms.

Now a blossoming youth on the verge of womanhood, she had lost none of her dexterity. From the safety of her perch, she squinted through the flickering light. Orange-yellow splashes of clarity sliced through the onyx night. Moments of luminescence revealed gauzy shapes roiling in the turbid darkness. Sharp cries pierced the stillness, announcing the unfolding scene.

The rabble dragged Esmene, flailing and shrieking, from the house. The priest grabbed her hoe, cracked its handle across his knee, and flung it aside. Arrosa's plump fist gripped one of Esmene's arms and Father Ricardo's gaunt fingers squeezed the other as they clutched the writhing woman.

Delicate bones, finely arched eyebrows and long lashes framing her black eyes gave Esmene the misleading appearance of fragility, but her ungovernable black hair better conveyed her dauntless spirit. Though Esmene was still young, relentless toil and the weight of worry had begun to erode her face as a three-day rain wears gullies into a woodland path.

"Where's Amika, that brat of yours?" Arrosa growled.

"The devil's spawn," Father Ricardo hissed. "The daughter of a witch is also a witch, polluted from birth by her mother's devil-dealing."

"She's not here," Esmene spat her defiant words at the priest. "You won't find her, so don't bother looking."

"Very well," Arrosa grumbled. "We'll make sure she doesn't come back. Luis, the rest of you, you know what to do." She turned and seized a torch from one of the men. With a strong arm, she swung it toward the simple hut. The other torch-bearers followed her lead.

Sparks traced a graceful, arcing path through the darkness as the mob hurled their flares toward the thatched roof. The goat cried piteously. The chickens screamed as they rushed toward the door. A dozen onlookers cheered or growled like angry dogs baying at a treed fox.

Not everyone in the crowd was hostile. Around the periphery, a handful of disheveled old wives, roused from their sleep, shook their kerchiefed heads, and cast sidelong glances at each other. One woman in her middle years stood apart, leaning against her almost-grown son, an arm threaded through the crook of his elbow. She covered her mouth with a handkerchief, eyes bulging in horror. She tried to stifle her revulsion, but one ragged sob escaped her constricted throat.

"What was that?" Marco Mendoza's hoarse voice rose above the virulent background noise. His head whipped around searching the crowd. "Who dares cry for a devil-worshipper?" His lips, pressed into a rigid line, slashed across his face as he pivoted around, searching the crowd. "Do we have another witch among us?"

The terrified woman clutched her son's arm more tightly. The youth was tall but as thin as a willow switch in winter. He wore the undyed gray habit of a Benedictine postulant. Its pointed cowl hung down the middle of his back. A heavy rosary dangled from a knotted rope belted around his waist. He struggled to compose his face, barely managing to conceal his churning stomach and pounding heart behind a mask of impassivity. He knew the woman now being manhandled by the angry crowd.

When he was a young boy, his ailing mother had sent him to Esmene's door. He remembered her kindness when she had seen him there, shuffling his feet in the dust.

"My mother sent me," he had announced awkwardly as he studied the dirt at his feet. "She has a bad stomach. I can hear it grumble. But it's not hunger," he explained. When he lifted his eyes, he saw a petite woman with sable hair and eyes. A sturdy young girl of about four years with a face as round as a harvest moon and large, acorn-brown eyes peeked from behind a bunched fistful of her mother's skirt. The woman had disappeared into her hut and emerged with a small packet. She spoke to him tenderly.

"Tell your mother to make an infusion with this." Esmene handed the packet to him.

"What is this?" He turned the bundle in his palm to examine it.

"It's a balm of ginger and turmeric. Tell her to prepare an infusion with these. I'm sure she'll feel better quickly."

Now, this image from his past swam through his pool of memories. He could hardly believe he was seeing that kindly woman accused of witchcraft. Since when had healing become so dangerous, he wondered.

"No point in wasting good food." Father Ricardo turned his attention to Esmene's animals. "Take the animals." He nodded in Arrosa's direction. "Heaven knows, we have plenty of poor, hungry people to feed, as the Lord commanded us to do." Arrosa and the priest held each other's eyes long enough for Arrosa to decipher Father Ricardo's meaning. The only bellies to be filled would be those of Arrosa and her family.

Amika clutched her gray wool cloak more tightly around herself as she trembled in the arms of the beech tree. Esmene's heels traced shallow furrows through the dirt as they dragged her away. Her mother had warned Amika this might happen. She knew there would be trouble when Marco and Andressa Mendoza's fourth child, their only son, was born with a frightfully deformed mouth. His upper lip did not come together in the middle, leaving a ghastly gap. Horrified villagers turned their heads when Andressa passed by, holding her baby. They surreptitiously touched forehead, shoulders, and heart, making the Christian sign of the cross to ward off evil. Andressa was a capable, experienced mother and quickly adapted to her baby's

3

needs, holding him upright when the pathetic infant nursed, so milk would not run out of his nose or dribble down his chin. Though she loved him as she did her other children, she knew people's aversion to his appearance would make his life lonely and difficult.

Andressa's husband, Marco, a temperamental Italian prone to hot rages, had lashed out when he saw the ravaged face of his long-awaited son. Desperate to place blame for this catastrophe on someone, he visited Father Ricardo.

"I can find no reason for this," Marco Mendoza whined to the priest. "Our other children are fine, perfect in every way. Why has God cursed us?"

"Are you sure it is God who has cursed you?" Father Ricardo asked, eyebrows arching almost to his hairline. "Have you been true to the Holy Church of Rome?"

"I am from Siena. You know that. Everyone in my country follows the teachings of the Roman Church, unlike some of the savages here who won't give up their old ways." Marco sniffed defensively.

"Do you know anyone who bears ill will toward you or Andressa?" Father Ricardo tapped the tip of his pointed chin with a boney finger.

Marco stopped to consider the question. "Last year our goat wandered into Esmene's garden. Esmene found him nibbling the rhubarb leaves. She dragged the poor animal back to our yard. She warned Andressa not to let our animals wander into her garden because some of her plants could be harmful." Marco paused, ruminating. He clenched his jaw, grinding it back and forth like a cow chewing its cud. "Shortly after that incident, Andressa's goat died. Andressa was livid. Nothing would calm her. She stalked into Esmene's yard and tore up all the rhubarb, and several other suspicious-looking plants as well—plants she had never seen in any other garden." The heat of his words fed the flames of his anger and brought a flush to his ruddy cheeks. "Yes, that's it!" he bellowed, so excited he nearly shouted, as the explanation dawned on him. "Esmene was angry that Andressa tore up her plants so she cursed our poor goat. And look at what has happened to us since then! Now we have a dead goat and a son with a mangled lip!"

"Yes, I have heard of this incident," Father Ricardo muttered, seemingly unmoved by Mendoza's passion. "Arrosa came to me. She said she witnessed the whole altercation from her yard and claimed Esmene was growing poisonous plants in her garden to aid in throwing hexes upon innocent people. In fact, she suspected Esmene purposely lured the goat into her dangerous yard."

"We must do something! We can't allow a devil worshiper to live among us," Mendoza fumed.

"Tomorrow I will go and inspect the garden myself, to determine if there is cause for concern." The priest stood, straightening his spine to accentuate his impressive height. Marco understood the interview was over. He pushed the rough woolen sleeves of his tunic up to his elbows, balled his fists, and stomped out the door.

The next day, Father Ricardo paid Esmene a visit. He found her stooped over a row of sweet peas crawling over a delicate trellis, a simple affair of her own making, made with hemp twine threaded between the top and bottom rails of a willow frame. He inhaled deeply as his eyes ran over the staggering bounty of Esmene's raised triangular beds. The long base of one triangle abutted the pointed end of the one next to it, creating a pattern of narrow, zigzag paths. Every plant was accessible from the pathways, so there was no need to trample them.

A symphony of fragrances made music in the air. The tangy smell of dill, the woody scent of thyme, and the minty aroma of hyssop penetrated the cool summer morning. The garden's lush abundance of colors rivaled the richness of a bishop's ceremonial robes. A low mat of alyssum crawled around the perimeter of the flower bed, filling the air with a smell so sweet that Father Ricardo paused, tilted his head back, and closed his eyes to inhale. Purple spikes of hyssop mingled with noble whorls of lavender arrayed on downy stems. Tiny, daisy-like chamomile flowers stood on ferny stalks next to stately hollyhocks. The effect was intoxicating.

When she noticed the lanky priest Esmene rose and wiped her hands on her dirty apron.

"I wasn't expecting visitors." She bent a knee in a half curtsey, not knowing how to greet a priest outside of the church.

"Good morning, Senora," he intoned in the nasal drone he used for his sermons. "I've come to see your garden. Marco Mendoza and Venena Arrosa have expressed concern about what you grow here."

"Really? No one has ever shown any interest in my garden." She sounded puzzled. "It's not very different than any other kitchen plot."

"I see you grow more than vegetables," he replied. His head swiveled like a weathervane on his long neck as he looked around. "Would you be so kind as to give me a tour?"

"I'd be happy to," Esmene said. She studied him, trying to read his intentions. A pang of anxiety tightened her throat, but pride soon overcame her reticence. "It's actually quite simple. In this raised bed there are flowers, as you can see—alyssum, marigolds, foxglove, and of course yarrow and chamomile." Esmene smiled proudly as she warmed to the guided tour.

Father Ricardo glanced nonchalantly around the garden.

"Here are the herbs—lavender, basil, thyme, sage, dill fennel, and hyssop." Esmene looked up at Father Ricardo's face, but it belied no emotion. How anyone could fail to appreciate the riot of color and cascade of scents, she wondered. "And of course, there are fruits over here—raspberries, strawberries, and my prize dwarf apple trees." Her upturned palm traced a wide arc over the triangular bed. "And here are the staple vegetables. Lentils, beans, carrots, turnips, squash, and of course cabbage for the winter months." She stopped, not wishing to harangue him with too much detail. "There are more, but this is the arrangement. Every plant is governed by its humors—hot or cold, wet or dry—as well as its personality, as people are. Some plants prefer the company of others, so I plant them together. And every plant has its use, sometimes many uses."

"Hmm," Father Ricardo mused. "Many uses, you say. Do they have both good and evil uses?"

Esmene's heart sank and her stomach clenched. This was surely a trap. Her mind replayed the recent unpleasant exchange she'd had with Andressa and Marco Mendoza. "People come to me asking for help to ease their discomforts, heal wounds, and alleviate internal problems like digestion and heart pain. I help them as best I can. As a good neighbor I can hardly turn them away if my plants can help them." She hoped her tone did not sound defensive or combative.

"And wouldn't prayer be more helpful? Only God wields the power over health and sickness, life and death," Father Ricardo challenged her.

"But the people who come to me have been praying most earnestly. If my plants can give them some relief, where is the harm?" Esmene countered. She stopped to take a deep breath, lowered the pitch of her voice, trying not to betray her rising alarm, and began again. "Our village is small. The nearest monastery hospice is a two-day hike from here. Though the monks are God's own hands on the sick, they practice bloodletting. Many of the hill people do not hold with the spilling of blood as a cure for anything. For untold generations, they have sought help from people like me, keepers of the ancient knowledge." She suddenly felt she had said too much and looked down at the dirt walk between the neat beds.

"Hmmm, is that right?" It was a statement, not a question. "The ancient knowledge." A sneer lifted one corner of his mouth. "So, your knowledge goes back to pagan times, before our Holy Mother Church saved us from the ways of the devil. Is that what you're saying?"

"Well, no." She paused, momentarily confused. "Well yes, I guess the ancient knowledge does go back that far. But it is practical

7

medicine, and it works for people. It has nothing to do with the devil. These plants were also created for our use by our most gracious God. People trust me and rely on me." Esmene sighed deeply and looked straight into Father Ricardo's face, his eyes as flat as a lizard's. She knew he had already reached his conclusion. She watched his neck stiffen.

"Yes, I see," Father Ricardo's eyes rolled down his long nose until his gaze rested on the diminutive gardener before him. "And do they trust that you will not cast curses when you have a grudge against them? You stand accused of cursing Marco and Andressa Mendoza's goat." Now his voice boomed as though he was addressing a crowd. "But even that was not enough to quell your seething anger, so you also cast a hex upon their innocent baby!"

"No! That's not true! Is that what they told you? That goat was eating rhubarb. That is why it died. And the baby," she sputtered to a halt. "That poor child. I'm very sorry for his defect, but it had nothing to do with me, I swear."

"Fine." Venom dripped from his lips. "If not you and your pagan medicine, then what other explanation is there?" Again, it was not a question. With that, Father Ricardo spun on his heel and marched out of the garden as stiff as a king's guardsman.

Within two days he had dispatched a letter to the bishop, pressing charges of witchcraft against her. The letter was merely a formality. Esmene's guilt was a foregone conclusion. No one would question Father Ricardo's judgment. The court was made up of self-styled defenders of the faith, privileged sons of rich men whose only interests were in defending their privileges and pursuing worldly pleasures. Esmene's life would be worth less than the bitter kale she grew in her garden. Mother and daughter could only pray, fearing what lay ahead. They were not surprised when the haughty priest and some of the neighbors marched through the night to her door. Their malicious cries of "heretic, devil-worshipper" rang out above the sizzling roar of her hut being consumed by fire.

Curled in the crotch of her beech tree, Amika watched the cinders of her life shoot into the slate sky. Eventually, the angry voices faded to silence. The trickling stream, trilling crickets, and moaning bullfrogs reclaimed the soundscape of the night.

Despite herself, toward morning Amika dozed. Scraps of her former existence filled her dreams, taunting her fitful sleep. In the misty half-light of early morning, before the brightening horizon signaled the return of the day, Amika slid down the mottled green-gray trunk of her tree. Tears seeped from her sleepy eyes as she surveyed the charred remains of her life. Existence had not always been so precarious for Amika and Esmene. Once they had lived in peace. Once their family had been whole.

1249
SPRING

Esmene knelt in the dirt of her kitchen garden. Urgency prodded her to finish her planting quickly. Spring had arrived late that year. Winter had been cold and long. Like a jealous lover spurned by his heartthrob, it refused to loosen its grip and give way to its tenderhearted rival, spring. Finally, the cornsilk-yellow sun had loosened winter's fingers. By late spring, the gentle sun no longer caressed the back of Esmene's neck but raked its hot nails over it, reddening her flesh.

After hours of bending over her herbs and vegetables, she stood, placed one hand on the small of her back, and stretched, lifting her face to the sky. Though small and slim, she was nonetheless a strong and vigorous woman. Her large, nearly black eyes contrasted sharply with her pale skin. The effect was striking. Her high cheekbones and thin lips were etched so precisely they could have been carved from ivory.

That morning, knowing she would be kneeling in the garden soil for hours, she had confined her lush black hair in a tightly wound linen headwrap that created a plump bun at the nape of her neck. Her daughter, Amika, a sturdy child of six years, hunted for beetles among bean plants. Her large, wide-set eyes, long lashes, and round face mimicked her father's, as did her robust little body. The resemblance was more than skin deep. The child's relentless kindness, outward displays of affection, and plain silliness were his also. Every day the girl reminded Esmene of all the reasons she loved her husband, Fermin, so much.

Esmene bustled over to the girl squatting in front of a resinous plant. She knelt at Amika's side and carefully wiped each of her little fingers with her apron "Amika, you must stay away from that pennyroyal! You do not want the oil to rub off on your skin. You are so small that even a small amount may make you dizzy." Clusters of purple flowers arranged themselves along a tall square stem. "This plant is useful. It can kill insects and keep fleas away. But it is also very powerful. You must not touch it."

Early that morning she had watched as Fermin shuffled off to tend the family's small field on the outskirts of the village. A buttery, early-morning sun shimmered against the cobalt sky in the rarified mountain air. The peaks of the Pyrenees to the north aspired to touch heaven, while the valley's ambition was to cradle and nurture the crops, the flocks, and the people.

The villager's farm plots stepped down a steeply terraced slope above the village. Centuries of Fermin's ancestors had labored to transform the hillside from dense forest into a tidy farm ringed with trees where Fermin tended barley, wheat, and broomcorn. Esmene and Fermin thought themselves lucky to own a modest hut, a patch of tillable soil, and a prolific garden. They felt equally blessed by their deep devotion to each other and their profound love for their little daughter, Amika.

"*Amika,*" she sighed as she watched her daughter poking and prodding the garden plants. *My daughter is stretching out. Her round baby face is no longer as plump as plenty. It won't be very many years until she is a young woman.*

The day had been a happy one. Amika was learning about plants, the blessing of God's third day of creation. She had decided to honor Amika's efforts with a "big girl" gift, a necklace plaited from Esmene's own hair. Amika engulfed her mother with an enthusiastic hug, so vigorous it squeezed the breath out of Esmene's lungs.

"I'll wear it every day," she enthused. "I'll never take it off."

Standing in her garden, Esmene allowed her mind to drift off, remembering days when Amika was a tiny baby. Involuntarily, a vision swam before her of Fermin scooping up their chubby baby, his large hands enveloping her tiny body, holding her far above his head and turning in circles. Amika's laughter fell like precious rain on

11

parched earth. She remembered the preternatural softness of her baby's fairy-thin brown hair, and the milky sweetness of her scent. Esmene treasured the memory of Amika exploring her glorious garden. Even before the baby could talk, Esmene gently repeated the names and uses of the plants, making up rhymes and songs to help the little girl remember.

Milk comes from Mummy, Mint's for the tummy
Tansy's for cough, but Mandrake—hands off!

Esmene reluctantly cut her daydreaming short. She and Fermin had agreed to meet at the church at midday to practice their dances for the festival of Saint Fermin. Saint Fermin was both Fermin's patron saint and the namesake of their region. The parish Church was the beating heart of the village. She and Fermin had been married there. Simple and austere as it was, with its thick granite walls and barrel-vaulted ceiling, it had held the hopes, prayers, and sorrows of the villagers for generations. On foggy nights, the priests rang its lone bell to guide travelers through the mountain passes to the safety of the village.

Many celebrations that punctuated the grinding labor of survival played out in its plaza. Spirited competitions—tugs of war, ram fights, wood chopping, and sawing—tested the strength of hard-working men and beasts. Herdsmen who tended cattle on the hillsides drove an assortment of cows of every description, youthful heifers to ancient matriarchs with full udders, down from their pastures and through the rutted path that bisected the village. Hilarity erupted as the poor, confused animals trotted or waddled through the street, seeking the nearest exit back to their pastures. Boys festooned in red neck scarves darted among them to display their bravery.

After the spectacle with the running cows, the villagers turned their attention to more serious business. The huge bulls, accustomed to a solitary life in mountain meadows among their harems, were herded to the edge of town. The master of ceremonies sounded his ram's horn trumpet. And they were off! Men wagered on which bull would run the fastest through the narrow village streets. The most foolhardy, full of youthful invincibility and an urgent need to prove their manliness, flung themselves into the race. Legs churned as they tried to stay just ahead of the charging bulls. Not all of them were successful, but even their injuries signified courage.

Some of the rituals sank their roots into the soil of the deep past, growing from the legends of the ancestors, people who had lived in these remote mountain villages for millennia. Echoes of the ancient culture pervaded even the holiest of Christian holidays. During the shortest days of winter, dancers with sheepskins and cowbells entwined around their waists carried lighted flares and marched through the village to scare away the darkness. Behind them, a good-hearted, pipe-smoking farmer with pants tucked into his socks, a black beret, and shepherd's staff paraded through the streets, distributing small treats to the children.

No revel would be complete without the dances. There were dances for women only, for men only, and for couples. This would be the first year Esmene and Fermin would dance together. Men and women danced, arms waving like wind-whipped branches. Their feet flew through complex dance steps. A two-man team pounded the butts of their sticks on an assembly of different-size planks. Each plank made a different, bell-like tone. Joyous music echoed off the stone buildings and resonated through the mountains. Esmene and Fermin knew their life together would be hard but infused with soul-nourishing moments of joy.

Years flowed on seamlessly. The reassuring cadence of the seasons swayed them from winter to summer like a mother rocking her baby's cradle. They were a proud people, with a unique culture far older than any other. Their people sprang from this very earth at the beginning of time.

The little family—Esmene, Fermin, and Amika—savored their security until one summer day when Fermin did not return from the fields. A savory stew simmered over the banked fire. Chunks of lamb, small red potatoes, onions, and carrots swam in a broth tinted fiery red by a pinch of precious Spanish paprika. Esmene envisioned Fermin's smile when he ducked his head under the lintel. She anticipated his delight when the smells of thyme, bay leaf, and oregano wafted toward him. But he did not walk through the door. Hours passed. A wicked, shrieking wind whipped up from the valley, confusing the gathering clouds. The bright yellow line between dark earth and cloudy sky paled to a ghostly gray. Jagged shards of lightning like broken glass menaced the heavens into quivering helplessness. The lamb stew cooled. The fire died a slow death as Esmene gathered Amika into her arms and wept. The following morning, she assembled a few neighbors and walked up the beaten path to their plot. Fermin lay splayed face down on the muddy ground, his right hand still gripping his hoe. A gnarled gall oak, gashed in half by lightning, lay across his back. That day the world shifted on its axis for Esmene and Amika.

CHAPTER TWO

1250

SUMMER

Amika woke to the scent of charred wood and thatch. Her brain reeled as it tried to make sense of her odd circumstances, tucked among the branches of her beech tree. Tears oozed from her eyes as dreamy visions of her happy childhood evaporated with the morning fog. Fear, then panic, replaced her reveries. Would they come looking for her? Where could she go?

She had little time to wonder. The dawn chorus of birds, joyously singing hymns of praise to the morning, struck a note of hope. But it did not last long. The intermingled songs of wagtails, and woodpeckers, bullfinches, and buntings ebbed to an unnatural silence. In their place, urgent alarm calls flowed through the woods like a wave of wails spreading the news of approaching danger. Before the sun had dissipated morning's foggy shroud, she could hear her vindictive neighbors drawing nearer.

"We've snared one witch." Amika recognized Marco's Italian accent. "Now we must find her young mutt. How did she slip away?"

"I never saw her. She must have run for her worthless life," Gorka, an undersized, timid slip of a man added. He would have loved to avoid this hunt but feared being branded a coward. He had already endured a lifetime of taunts.

"Father Ricardo says it's not worth the trouble to send the witch to court in Pamplona. They would undoubtedly convict her, based on his word alone. Why bother? We can build a pyre as well as anyone. If we can find the girl, it will be just as easy to roast two shanks as one. We'll save firewood." Marco chuckled.

15

"We don't have forever to find her," Gorka countered. "Father Ricardo says if we can't find the girl, her mother will become tinder tomorrow in any case. Keeping Esmene around can only cause unrest. She's not without friends, you know."

"Enough talk!" a brawny peon interrupted. Bardol, a broad-shouldered, beetle-browed hulk of a man scowled. "Spread out and don't stop looking until we find her."

Amika could not endure listening any longer. The overheard conversation cudgeled her with the force of a well-swung ax. She dropped to the ground and disappeared into the familiar forest.

I must think of a way to reach my mother, Amika thought. *Where would they be keeping her? She must be at Venena Arrosa's house. Father Ricardo would not want to arouse suspicion by harboring an unmarried woman at his house.*

Amika lurked around the periphery of the village, keeping out of sight until the feeble light of a bleak day melted into a puddle of tragic darkness. The disappointed searchers returned to their huts. When darkness descended, Amika glided into town as noiselessly as an owl in flight. The dogs knew her smell, so did not bark. Only a stray rooster squawked an alarm.

Venena Arrosa's hut was even poorer than Amika's had been. Its thatch was blackened with mold; one stone wall bowed out, threatening to collapse. Like Amika's hut, the only entryway was a single door. In front of the door the burly peasant, Bardol, planted his feet like the roots of an oak. Unsleeping, unblinking, with a mind innocent of all thought, he stared into the night. Despair crushed hope from Amika's soul, but she did not retreat. Though she was as powerless as a kitten under a horse's hooves, she waited, hidden in the tangle of Arrosa's untended vines.

Early the next morning, before the mists lifted, Arrosa lumbered out her door, embracing a bundle of kindling as if it were a babe in arms.

"Let me help you with those," Bardol offered.

Arrosa, flattered by the attentions of this burly young man, demurely handed him her bundle and together they walked toward the square.

Amika slunk into the hut like a ghostly shadow.

"Mother," she whispered into the gloom.

Esmene materialized out of the darkness. "Go! You must go at once. If they find you here, you know what they will do," she hissed.

Amika grabbed her mother's wrist and, with the strength of a man, dragged her toward the door. She had gotten only a few steps when Esmene jerked to a stop. "You can't," Esmene murmured. "They've tethered me like a dog. You can't free me. Now go! I demand it."

"I can't leave you here."

"You must! I insist." Their eyes met. "Truly, Amika, there is no virtue in getting both of us killed."

Amika knew her mother was right. As she had done the night before, she did as her mother ordered and melted back into the fog. She watched from the church bell tower in despair as townspeople brought their contributions of kindling for the human sacrifice about to take place in the plaza of Saint Fermin's church. The atmosphere prickled with guilty pleasure. The mood was almost festive.

All eyes were riveted on the unfolding drama in the plaza. No one saw Amika enter a side door that led up the rickety stairs to the choir loft, then up another flight to the bell tower.

Father Ricardo stood before a thick beechwood branch planted vertically in the plaza, dressed in his richest vestments, reciting the requiem prayers for the dead. "*Requiem aeternam, dona eis, Domine, et lux perpetua luceat eis.*" Eternal rest grant unto her, O Lord, and let perpetual light shine upon her.

The fleshy peon, Bardol, dragged Esmene by her tether through the street. She stumbled but did not fall. Her vacant eyes looked as if death had already taken her. She shuffled along with as

17

much dignity as she could summon. Bardol pushed her back up against the stake. He wrapped nine coils of stout hemp rope firmly around her. A torch blazed in a hastily constructed sconce. Arrosa was the first to deposit her armful of kindling at Esmene's feet. People, many of whom had been her friends and neighbors, followed Arrosa's example until the heap of tinder reached Esmeme's thighs. Only then did she panic. Looking desperately into their eyes she berated the people.

"You know me! I have helped you. You trusted me. I never harmed a soul." They placed their bundles at her feet, not lifting their gazes to her face, turning their backs, and silently slinking off.

Father Ricardo closed his prayer book and handed it to an acolyte. "Do you confess your sins? Do you plead for forgiveness for your apostasy?" Though his words were meant for Esmene, he faced the crowd.

"I am innocent! If I said otherwise, I would be making a false confession." Her voice became shrill. "You know it, and God knows it!" Then she loudly began reciting her own prayer. "Our Father who art in heaven."

"Silence! Satan himself puts these words into her mouth," Father Ricardo said.

"Hallowed be thy name."

"Silence! No more of this!" Father Ricardo withdrew the torch from its sconce and touched its flame to the pile of tinder.

A ghastly scream pierced the air. Heads twisted around searching for the source of the other-worldly howl. It had not come from Esmene, who continued praying her "Our Father." It reverberated through the crowd from above.

The flames flared up around Esmene, not creating the slow burn Father Ricardo had envisioned, but exploding into a fireball. Immediately the fire sucked every whiff of air from around the stake. Deprived of oxygen, Esmene lost consciousness before the flames could consume her. Her body hung from the stake like drying laundry from a clothesline. The fire recovered its breath and resumed clawing its way to the stake. But Esmene was already gone.

The ghoulish sound came again, this time resounding like a single syllable flung into the universe. "Noooooo!"

"What is that? What made that ungodly screech?" The people looked around nervously.

"That's Satan leaving her body," Father Ricardo asserted.

The townspeople stole glances at each other.

"What if she was not guilty?" Andressa Mendoza whispered into Marco's ear.

"Did you see? She died before the flames could torment her."

Soon the charred remains, no longer recognizable as a human being, stared at them, mutely accusing them of burning an innocent friend and neighbor. A ripple of horror pulsed through the crowd. They returned to their homes, closed their doors against the crackling of the dying embers, and did not open them again that day, nor the next. A dull ache settled over them, along with the falling ashes of the pyre.

No one noticed Amika as she snuck from the bell tower and out of town. She did not stop walking until she had disappeared into the damp, gray wilderness of the forest. She walked, then she ran as if running could distance her from the nightmare she had just witnessed.

She abandoned the well-trodden track up the mountain and walked deliberately into the underbrush. Her lungs heaved. Scratches scored her arms. A jumble of dewy ferns soaked her cloak as she pressed deeper into the mist. She slipped on moss-camouflaged rocks. Trees scattered themselves across the landscape like a disorderly army deserting the battlefield. By the time she slowed to a stop, the deep forest loomed in total silence around her. Her dress clutched at her ankles as she pivoted in a circle, searching for a safe shelter. The malevolent forest peered down at her from all sides, waiting to ensnare her with its creeping vines.

With no plan or destination, she simply walked. Hunger accompanied her, urgently poking her ribs as she tried to ignore its insistent nagging. By afternoon, her stomach felt hollow, her limbs were leaden, and her head was light. By evening, an urgent thirst overwhelmed her hunger. She strained, trying to detect the sound of running water. There was none. With the little strength that was left to her, she knelt and haphazardly folded all the ferns within arm's reach toward her knees, curled up among them in her sodden woolen cloak, and lost herself too exhausted oblivion.

Muted by the deep mist, dawn crept in almost imperceptibly. Amika was reluctant to awaken as the forest around her came to life. She squeezed her eyes closed and pulled her damp cloak more tightly around herself. She dozed in a semiconscious morning stupor. Sleep abandoned her when threads as delicate as corn silk tickled her face. Reluctantly she opened her eyes. A pair of amber eyes filled her field of vision a thumb's length away from her nose. Fine whiskers grazed her cheek. She froze. A moment later a miniature paw reached out and tapped her nose. She jerked involuntarily and the fox kit that had been examining her face let out a cry of alarm more like a chipmunk's yelp than a dog's bark. It trotted off a short distance but did not run away. Amika held the pup's gaze for one more magical moment before it trotted away into the morning mist.

Her head swam as she sat up. Her stomach felt as if rocks tumbled inside it. Her tongue was as thick and coarse as a bottle brush. She groaned. The forest awakened. Birds and red squirrels chattered, spreading the news of the day.

Her agonized, headlong dash had taken her into an area of the forest that was totally unfamiliar to her. Arching her back, she peered upward and saw tiny patches of dusky sky winking through the overstory.

She conjured visions of forays into the forest with her mother, searching for mushrooms beneath soggy leaves. The forest canopy of her memory was a benevolent grandmother whose ancient face smiled down on them. Esmene had made a treasure hunt of it, challenging Amika to find colorful rocks bathing in the rivulets. Amika had loved taking off her shoes and wading in the ice-melt cold water streaming off the mountains. She proudly presented her mother with handfuls of colorful pebbles.

Now, Amika found herself in alien surroundings. Almost no sun reached the ground here. The vestiges of indigo gentians and tiny alliums skittered across the forest floor, their flowers wilted now that leaves had unfolded to block their sun. She recognized very few of the food plants she and her mother had hunted. Amika tried to summon her recollections of the forest as she remembered it.

First, I must find water and an opening in the canopy. There I will find food, Amika reasoned. Her head cleared a bit and she lurched to her feet, listening intently. To her right, she heard the vague spluttering of running water. She waited until the earth stopped swaying and her blurred vision resolved itself into a single image, then slogged through the ferns in the direction of the hoped-for water. Her body, weakened by hunger, was less than enthusiastic about the project. She ignored her bloodied feet, unprotected since she had lost her leather slippers in the urgency of her escape.

Water! She flung herself belly down on the cool mat of mosses that lined the banks of the brook and plunged her face into the stream. A bright patch hinting of an opening in the overstory drew her like a siren's song. As she followed the rivulet upstream, the tall forest trees tapered to brushy willows surrounding a small, rocky glade.

She wandered the verge between forest and meadow, searching for familiar plants. Amika sunk to her knees for a closer look. The soft, pink petals of a dog-rose caught her eye. Here was food! Her mother had concocted delicious jams from fresh rose apples and made tea from the previous year's winter-softened fruit. Amika had never eaten them straight from the bush, but she was certain they were food. She plucked the tiny, fresh berries until all that remained were last year's desiccated ones. She plucked the petals from the blush-pink flowers and stuffed them into her mouth. They tasted surprisingly sweet except for the bitter white base. Amika sighed, squatted on her haunches, and inhaled deeply. The smell of damp earth, fallen leaves, and pine needles calmed her. A musky, spicy scent like celery drew her attention. In a muddy patch, she recognized the tall umbels of Angelica. She snapped a stem and sunk her teeth into the crisp stalk. It summoned memories of the celery in her mother's stew. She recognized the ferny leaves of yarrow among the grasses edging the glade. Its sweet, licorice-like scent belied the bitter, tangy taste of its leaves, but it was food.

Here is a place I can at least survive, she thought. The sweet comfort of pristine water and edible plants, however distasteful they might be, enticed her to stay all day. That night she returned to the safety of the hushed forest and cuddled down in her ferny bed. Most animals shunned the deep woods. She shared its dark recesses only with an industrious woodpecker on the trunk of an oak whose staccato tapping rang through the woods, and with a family of foxes. Early the next morning the amber-eyed pup she had met the first night introduced his brothers and sisters. A disordered mob of seven kits watched as their brother once again awakened the sleeping stranger with his gentle tap. It was not long before she could recognize each of the kits individually. She named the pup who discovered her Pussy Paws. It was not a very dignified name, but his dainty, white-tipped feet with their retractable claws reminded her of a cat. Soon, the unruly troop took no more notice of her than of the burgeoning mushrooms as they tussled in the ferns, tumbling over each other in mock battles.

One rose-colored evening after another day tramping through the glade in search of edibles, she encountered the tattered remains of her leather slipper, now reduced to a useless strip of leather. The next morning when he awakened her, she dangled it in front of Pussy Paws. Ever curious, he gingerly danced closer, stretching his pointed snout toward the leather. She suspended it just out of his reach as he jumped to catch it. Amika wrapped the remnant around a smooth, palm-size knob of wood and tossed the ball into the forest. She laughed as the pup chased it. The startling sound of her laughter reminded her how alone she was. Pussy paws chomped down and violently thrashed his head back and forth. as if trying to kill a vole. The seven siblings noticed Pussy Paws frolicking, and soon all of them were competing for possession of the strip of leather. For the first time, Amika noticed the vixen keeping vigilant watch from the shelter of shrubs bordering the glade. Playing with the pups became a cheerful daily ritual.

Through the summer she kept herself alive by adding new plants to her diet. As the days shortened, the plants dried and wrinkled like old men, and sank back into their roots, taking shelter until spring summoned them forth once more. She knew she could not last the winter in this place. She would need a more permanent shelter. The family of foxes changed their habits too. With prey becoming scarcer, the troupe dispersed to seek their territories. The cheery aura they created disappeared, leaving her dejected. The familiar hunger pains returned and, with them, dire anxiety. Her cloak, now torn and frayed, was still her only refuge from chilly nights.

The harvest gold autumn light gave her some small hope of a mild winter. She set off to the south, away from the high peaks that cloaked themselves in their wintery blanket more each day. Hunger pursued her. Some days she found no food at all. Some days she grubbed slugs from the undersides of fallen logs and scraped lichens from the rocks. She could think only of food. Hunger pangs transmuted into chronic, agonizing pain. Energy drained from her like milk from an overturned bucket. Eventually, she could barely move and wanted nothing more than to sleep. One late autumn night she found a shallow cavity under a ledge of rock. She curled up and prayed the bears and wolves that had terrorized her dreams would come to claim her. Each night she prayed this would be her last.

Just before dawn, after another long night of teeth-chattering cold, she dreamed that a hand stroked her tangled hair then brushed rough knuckles against her cheek.

"Mother? Have you come to take me home?" she mumbled in her delirium.

"No, child. I am not your mother."

With difficulty, Amika opened her eyes to an apparition— an old woman, backlit by the dawn's light. Wild white hair radiated from her head like a halo. The only features Amika could discern were two sparkling eyes ringed with a network of wrinkles as intricate as a spider's web.

"But I will take you home," she whispered. With that, she gripped Amika's arm and draped it across her humped shoulder, wrapped her other arm around Amika's waist, and dragged her to her feet. The girl weighed as much as a ten-year-old, though judging by her height, the older woman guessed she must be older, perhaps an adolescent.

The next time Amika awoke, the smell of porridge roused her. She jerked to a sitting position and tried to crawl to the pot suspended over an open hearth.

"No, girl. You are not ready to eat. Your body will reject any food you try to give it. First, you must drink." She offered Amika an airy tea with hints of apple and flowery sweetness.

"Chamomile tea is good for digestion and will prepare your stomach for food," The old woman said in a voice as dark and smooth as velvet.

"Who are you?" Amika croaked. She had not used her voice in so long that the throaty sound of her own speech startled her.

"No need to worry, girl," the crone replied. "This is my home. You are safe here." The old woman took Amika's cup away and replaced it with a wooden bowl of porridge of ground barley and sweetened with wild honey. The nutty flavor and slightly chewy texture revived Amika.

"My name is Ane. And yours?" the old woman asked.

"Amika," she answered. not raising her eyes from the bowl.

The crone watched her intently, noting her tattered cloak, her matted, filthy hair, her scratches, and bruises. All these told a story, but the climax of this story was her emaciated body. Clearly, this girl had been alone and barely surviving for months.

Amika finally pried her eyes from her bowl and raised her head. "Thank you," she whispered.

The woman she originally took to be ancient looked younger at a closer range. Though the nimbus of wiry white hair created a corona around her head, it was neither dirty nor unkempt. Her deeply lined, heart-shaped face bespoke a rough outdoor life, yet it was somehow beautiful, with its wide forehead and long, straight nose. Its most startling feature was intense, lustrous brown eyes, so clear and shimmering they seemed to project light.

"Where are we?" Amika murmured as if talking to herself. She craned her neck, peering around the dark interior of Ane's hut. She had never seen a house like this. It seemed to grow out of the earth like a hummock among tree roots. It was irregularly circular with a shallow, domed ceiling of woven branches covered by a sod roof. Tentacle roots, like fine lace, snaked through the sod. Palm prints covered the walls where Ane had patted clay plaster onto the walls. An iron pot hung over an open clay hearth nestled in a corner. A low seat made from the crux of a juniper stump squatted in the center of the room and an assortment of poorly made baskets lined the walls. Two rabbit pelts hung splayed against the wall.

"You are safe here, girl. You stumbled into my haven. I found you tucked under a rock ledge like a hibernating hedgehog and brought you here," the crone chuckled.

Amorphous images floated at the edges of Amika's memory. The hunger and cold came flooding back. She shivered involuntarily at the recollection.

"Where are you from, dear girl?" Ane asked.

"I have no home to return to. They, they ..." Amika's voice broke. "They took my mother and burned her and our house. They are coming for me." Amika's breath came in gasps. Panic overwhelmed

25

her reason. Her eyes darted wildly around the room. She stood up and dashed for the low doorway.

Ane caught her wrist before she could escape. "Be calm. There is no danger here. There will be plenty of time to tell your story. You need not speak of it now."

"You will not put me out? I cannot pay you. I have nothing to give."

"No, girl. The Old Ones do not make mistakes. They must have sent you to me for a reason. Now you must rest and regain your strength. The days grow short. We will need to put up more food if we both intend to eat through the coming winter." A benevolent smile graced her face.

I am saved. Amika sighed. She closed her eyes and slept. Howling wolves and sparking torches did not torment her dreams.

CHAPTER THREE
1250
WINTER

The wind whistled as it battered the earthen hut. Cold air seeping in through the walls chilled baskets of carrots, leeks, and wild potatoes that lined the interior. Bundled herbs and grains hung from the ceiling.

The plants in Ane's small garden hibernated under a quilt of snow like the dormice who coiled themselves up and slept snugly in mossy dens until spring tickled them back to life. Amika thought this a good idea and wished she could simply curl up until spring. But there was work to be done if they were to survive the cold months.

A pale winter sun cast its sidelong glance across the landscape, causing crystalline sparkles to dance across the powdery new snow. Shimmering gems sparkled on every bough. Amika and Ane peeked through thin slits cut across the kerchiefs they tied around their faces to protect their eyes. Wool leggings swaddled their calves as they lumbered through snow as fine as flour. They stopped at a spot where a dwarf juniper sprawled among a tumble of rocks. A colorful clique of Bohemian waxwings gorging on juniper berries erupted from the bushes. Amika straightened and flung her arms wide, drinking in the sharp, almost scentless air. Only the juniper's peppery odor spiced the clean breath of winter.

"This is a perfect place," Ane said as she bent low to examine the juniper. "See the rabbit tracks? They have everything they need to survive the winter here. There are juniper berries and a few sprigs of green plants hidden in the rock crevasses to eat, the snow melted by their warm bodies to drink, and a marvelous hidey-hole for shelter." Ane brought energy and enthusiasm to the rabbit trapping expedition. In Amika, Ane glimpsed the beautiful young woman she had once been. The beauty that had laid itself on the supple surfaces of her youthful face and skin were gone now. They had sunk below the skin's surface, like spring leaves on water, to beautify her soul.

"Let's get to work. Amika, hand me a half dozen of those willow wands."

Amika watched as Ane bent several pliable twigs and bound them together with twine to fashion a small tunnel. She covered it with juniper branches and baited a twine snare with dried rosehip apples.

"There!" Ane wobbled to her feet, wiping her hands on her cloak. "The apples will be irresistible! We will return in a day or two. Be prepared to make rabbit stew," she announced confidently.

"I know how to make stew!" Amika chimed in.

Ane smiled, amused by Amika's youthful fervor. In fact, Amika had proved her worth in many ways in the months she had lived with Ane. The skills Amika had learned at her mother's hearth enriched Ane's austere diet. She could simmer their foraged mushrooms with leeks and basil, stew turnips with onions, garlic, and parsley. She discovered winter greens, ox-eye daisy leaves, hairy bittercress and prickly sow thistle hiding in protected pockets tucked up against south-facing rocks. The girl, Ane concluded, was in fact sent by Mari, queen of the goddesses, to enliven and enrich her old age. A sudden pang stabbed her heart as a memory of her lost daughter broke through the porous barrier between past and present.

***

Once Ane had a home and family like Amika's. They lived in a small town tucked into a snug valley along the Way of St. James where an ancient Roman bridge believed to have miraculous powers spanned the Arga river. The credulous local people believed that if you led any animal three times around the central pillar, the one that contained relics of Santa Quiteria, it would be protected from rabies. The people raised sheep and farmed the rocky soil as best they could. They also fed and sheltered travelers who walked the pilgrimage route to Santiago. In this way, the poor, who could not make the long trek to Santiago themselves, or purchase indulgences as the rich did, could expiate their sins and gain favor in heaven by feeding and sheltering the pilgrims.

Dense trees shaded the river Arga, flowing deep and fast between two high hills, making the water appear black. Knights Templar "guarded" the bridge, taking from pilgrims both rich and poor any possession they fancied as their toll.

Ane was only fourteen when it happened. One cloudless late-summer afternoon she and her father fanned out across the grassy hillside, driving the sheep down from the high summer slopes to their lower wintering grounds. They were a team. Unlike other fathers who would have given away the baby whose birth had killed his wife, Ane's father raised the girl as he would have raised a boy. He reared her to be a capable and self-sufficient partner.

Suddenly a feisty ewe and her nearly grown lamb bolted from the herd. Ander, their manly red dog with exceptional herding skills, lit out in pursuit. When neither dog nor sheep returned by late afternoon, her father ordered Ane to find them. She knew this land like she knew her own blameless hands. She strode down the hill toward the woody perimeter of the glade where her family's traditional pastures intersected the path to Santiago.

Two men squatted over the carcass of an eviscerated ewe, bloody hands holding fresh mutton impaled on their spears over a small open fire. A nearly grown lamb wailed nearby but would not leave its dead mother, and Ander would not leave the lamb. Ander snarled fiercely as one of the men approached. Snapping and growling, he kept the man at bay while driving the lamb uphill, away from the trail.

"Get rid of the damn dog," one of them snarled more viciously than any cur. Moments later, Ane watched helplessly as he threw a dagger through the dog's throat as accurately as a seamstress draws her needle through fine silk. A husky man darted toward the stunned lamb and grabbed its unbobbed tail. Unable to contain herself, Ane screamed in unison with the struggling lamb.

"What's this?" the knife-wielder smiled through his beard. "Another lamb for our consumption?" The others laughed at his witty analogy. Ane, though as innocent as grace itself, felt hot menace radiating from the man. He lumbered toward her, snatching her as easily as he would pick an apple from a tree. Kicking and tearing at his hair and beard with all her strength did nothing but inflame the brute. He threw her to the ground, smothering her with his full weight. She thought this would be the moment of her death. She welcomed it. She willed herself dead. She let her spirit drift away from her body. Her disembodied spirit gazed down at the girl struggling in the dust as if watching a stranger. Finally, she gave up the struggle and the Templar impaled her with his body's "sword," while the others laughed and cheered him on. When it was over, she stumbled back to her father, battered and bloodied.

He barely recognized the dazed child as his sweet daughter. He sensed immediately what had happened. "Who did this?" her father raged.

"I don't know. They were strangers. They wore white tunics painted with red crosses," Ane blubbered between sobs.

"Templars!" her father raged helplessly. "They are supposed to protect the Way against robbers, but they are little more than robbers themselves. They have the favor of the Papist Church. There is nothing we can do. They do as they will."

He looked away in shame. He had failed the primary duty of every father—to protect his child. Ane clung to his waist trembling and sobbing convulsively. He patted the piteous child's matted hair, violated and forlorn as she was.

Through winter, though only a girl herself, Ane expanded to proportions grotesque for one so young. Without the girl's mother to advise him, Ane's father hid her. In spring he called the wife of his most trusted friend and swore her to secrecy. In spring, she delivered Ane of a baby girl. Tender and pink, the baby was as fragile butterfly wings. When Ane's unformed breasts would not produce sufficient milk, the midwife showed her how to soak a rag in ewe's milk for the baby to suckle. The child lived until spring when a late ice storm brought a fever to the tiny infant. She gasped for breath. She struggled to suckle at the twisted milky rag. She fought against sleep, wailing through the long nights. It was a battle the babe could not win.

Ane and her father laid the miniature body in a dismal little grave outside the wall of the church's graveyard, as close to holy ground as an unbaptized newborn could be laid to rest. They sprinkled her tiny body with delicate paper-thin rock roses. Each pink blossom lasts only a single day, like the single season of the baby's life.

As they scooped the loose earth over her, a luminous white moonstone pendant emerged from the overturned soil. On it was carved a round face with closed eyes and a peaceful expression. Ane rubbed her thumb over its smooth surface until it shone. Perhaps it was a gift from another pair of grieving parents to their own dead baby. She tucked the pearly stone with its angelic face into the leather pouch she wore at her waist. Her baby's spirit would always be with her.

Ane mourned her still. She treasured Amika as if she were the granddaughter she might have had if her child had lived to have babies of her own. Ane never ceased to wonder at Amika's fortitude. Through the cold, hungry months Amika, restless with pent-up energy, made forays into the forest, ferreting out anything that might be useful. She searched for firewood in every sheltered cleft and from beneath fir trees, whose snow-laden branches bent low enough to kiss the ground. During long nights in the cold hut, the fog of their exhalations mingled as Amika and Ane shared their stories with each other.

For many years Ane had survived by trapping forest creatures and nurturing a spartan garden. Ane animated the crystalline winter nights with tales of the Old Ones, stories kept alive by retelling over hearth fires since ancient ancestors lived here at the foot of towering glaciers.

"Do you know the story of Mari?" Ane asked Amika.

"Yes, I think so." Reflections of sparks spinning upward from the fire glittered in Amika's eyes. "But please tell me again." She grinned in animated delight.

"Ama Lurra, the goddess we call Mari, shows herself as a beautiful woman dressed in an elegant red dress, but she can also appear as a ram, her favorite animal. She lives below the ground and emerges in caves. She is the goddess of justice and honesty. Her mighty power keeps the forces of nature in balance. Have you ever seen a bolt of lightning hurl itself across the sky without touching the earth?" It was a rhetorical question. Amika knew not to interrupt with an answer. "That was Mari bursting across the heavens in her cart pulled by four white horses. She is married to Sugaar, but they live apart because Mari's domain is the earth. When she shows herself she emerges in caves. Sugaar rules the sea. When they meet the earth and skies seethe with wild storms. Thunder is Sugaar's booming voice. Mari's passion torments the air with rain, hail, wild winds."

Amika, thrilled with the recollection of an old memory, could not contain herself. "Yes, I know this story! My mother filled my ears with stories of my father to keep his memory alive, and so that I should take pride in his strength and virtue. She told me my father sometimes went to the mouth of a cave to beg Mari to spare his crops from pelting hail." Ane smiled with forbearance at the interruption. "My mother disapproved, thinking that it was a pagan practice, but my father could not be persuaded to abandon the time-honored traditions of his family."

"Mari is very powerful." Ane picked up the thread and began again to weave her story. "All life, as well as all the other goddesses, come from Mari. She is the protector of the earth. In the beginning, darkness covered the earth. The people lived in darkness and were afraid of the evil spirits that threatened them in their shadowy land. They begged Mari to help. She wished to help them, so she gave birth to a daughter, Llargi Amandrea, Mother Moon. You can see

Amandrea's face when she turns to look toward the earth." Ane paused. "Have you seen her when you stared into the face of the moon?'

"Yes, I've seen a face in the full moon," Amika replied.

"Have you ever wondered what happens to you when you die?" Ane asked.

"Of course," Amika replied. "Our souls ascend a great stairway to heaven to dwell in the house of the Lord forever." She reverently dipped her head.

"Is that what your mother taught you?" Ane's asked in her soothing, velvety voice.

"God the Father lives in heaven. We go there to be with him unless we have lived an evil life. Then we go to Hell, where we are tortured forever." Amika dutifully parroted the catechism the priest had taught her, the same priest who tortured her mother to death.

"Is that the only story you were taught?" Ane persisted.

"Yes." Amika paused. "Well, most of the time. When I cried for my dead father, my mother comforted me with another story." She paused. Her unfocused gaze stared into the snapping fire. She drew a deep breath and began. "She told me when people die, their souls walk on a rainbow to the moon and remain there, in safety with the moon goddess, until they decide they want to return to the Earth to live another life. They return in the form of rain drops." Amika smiled tenderly. "This story comforted me more than thinking my father was beyond my reach forever. I have always welcomed the rain, believing I could feel the presence of my father."

"Interesting," Ane sighed. "The old ways have not disappeared completely, even where the priests terrorize the people with their fearsome religion." She trained her intense eyes on Amika again. "Do you want to hear more about the sun and the moon?"

"Yes, please go on."

"The people thanked Mari for the moon but pleaded for yet more light. So, the benevolent goddess gave birth to another daughter, Eguzki Amandrea, Mother Sun. To prevent rivalry between her daughters, she decided to divide time between the two of them. That is why we have both sun and moon. Life on earth depends on Mother Sun. She is the goddess who travels across the sky each day and sinks every evening into the red-tinged horizon returning to Mari, her mother. Then Mother Moon rises to conquer the night, sending evil spirits back underground. Evil witches and sorcerers lose their powers when her light touches them. She keeps us safe at night, but beware of moonless nights." Ane studied Amika's face to see if she understood her stories.

"I remember the sunflower mother nailed to our front door." Amika murmured. "She told me it was a symbol of the sun, meant to protect our house and bring good luck. Now I see it was more than that. Even though Mother did not speak of the ancient gods, she nonetheless sought the protection of Mother Sun. Still, she tried to be a good Christian. I think she followed the new religion because she was afraid of the priest." Amika's heart lurched with the memory of her mother being dragged away. "Please go on with your stories," Amika begged. "Living here in the forest with you makes the old tales seem real to me now."

Amika was rapt under the spell of Ane's stories. She reached out and gently touched the moon-faced ivory amulet Ane withdrew from her pouch.

"These moon-faced carvings used to be common, though not plentiful. They are offerings to Mari who lives underground. Grieving parents bury them with a baby when it dies and is consigned to the grave. I have another talisman I keep in my pouch." Ane withdrew an ornament carved from wood as hard as iron.

"What does this symbol mean?" Amika asked. The image looked like a four-leafed clover, except each petal, thin at the base and bulbous at the end, leaned to the right. "Is it a special god?"

Ane smiled. Her fingers curled around the carved ornament.

"I received this at the cave ceremony when I was a young woman like you. The four petals stand for the gods of water, earth, air, and fire." A shadow passed over her face. "Unlike the Christian crucifix that commemorates torture and death, this beautiful emblem symbolizes all the elements that makeup life."

Ane reached out and gently patted the girl's hand. "I think that's enough for tonight. The winter is long. We will have plenty of time to tell our stories. There are more legends and more gods and goddesses than you can imagine. The stories of our Old Ones are as ancient as the earth itself."

CHAPTER FOUR
1251
SPRING

Winter's melted memories coursed down rivulets into the creeks. Amika and Ane could see the weave at the bottoms of their baskets, now depleted of dried vegetables. The sun had not yet warmed the soil enough to nurture Ane's humble seeds. It would be many weeks before Amika could harvest nature's garden.

"The Old Ones called this time of year the starving time," Ane explained when Amika complained of hunger. "Spring is late this year, but we must trust Basajaun, the Lord of the Woods, to lead us to his hidden caches of edibles."

"Should I also pray to Jesus?" Amika asked.

Ane's pressed her lips tightly together and gave Amika a sidelong glance. "You may," she grumbled. "But you might be better served by praying to the goddess you call Mary. Jesus will have too many lives to look after if everyone appeals only to him."

"Jesus is all-seeing, all-knowing, and all-powerful." Part of Amika was somehow comforted by the catechism she had learned at her mother's knee.

Ane sighed. "Perhaps he is, but he may need our gods to help him tend to the details of life here on earth. There is no harm in appealing to both."

Amika nodded at the logic of this approach.

Hunger prodded Amika's ribs as she doggedly pursued food among winter's remains. Gaps between leafless branches riddled the forest canopy like a badly made basket, allowing mottled sunlight to reach the ground. Where light found its way to the soil, the dormant earth cradled small treasures. Amika poked her nose into every hidden corner where plants might have found refuge. Mushrooms hid under rocky ledges. Bright red rose hips glistened from beneath a scrim of ice. Tiny, dried seeds of last season's curly dock clung to the desiccated stalks. The dappled forest floor harbored wintergreen and purslane, dry and mealy when raw, but sweet when cooked. The low-lying glade smelled like a wet dog, a sign the earth was waking up from its winter's slumber. Though the boggy soil was still spongy, Amika found tightly coiled ferns ready to unfurl their lacy leaves. She dug in the grassy places for wild potatoes and onions.

"Come, girl," Ane called. "You should know about this plant." Ane led her to a brown rosette of winter-shriveled leaves.
"I know what this is!" Amika beamed. "My mother and I ... " she trailed off, her voice fading as the memory of her mother drained her enthusiasm. "We called it sorrel," she said quietly.

"Good," Ane said. She winced involuntarily, sharing Amika's pain. "Then I suppose you also know that even though its leaves are not edible now, its roots can be cooked, and the dry seeds are eaten raw." Ane looked pleased as Amika's eyes narrowed, inspecting the dried, lance-shaped leaves flattened to the damp ground. Like a miserly man, the hills yielded just enough to keep them alive but always teetering at the knife-edge of hunger.

Amika explored every inch of their small domain—glade, forest, stream, mountainside, and verdant meadows. As the weather warmed, Amika roamed farther, scouting remote hills and shadowy valleys. Like an adventurer on an expedition to never-before-seen lands, she delighted in encountering strange beasts unlike those she had seen near her village. Fat, shaggy mountain horses with large heads, short necks, and stubby legs roamed the hills. High, rocky crags sheltered chamois, a strange creature that looked as if it had been cobbled together from pieces of both goat and antelope. A dark brown band ran up its face from its muzzle through its eyes and ears.

Spring sun caressed Amika's shoulders tenderly as she stooped over the rocky ground, prodding every crevasse for hidden food. When she could crouch no longer, she straightened, stretched, and raised her eyes to the rocky heights. A marmot basking on a sunny rock greeted her with a piercing whistle. Amika smiled and tried to whistle in response but only sputtered through slack lips. She laughed at her pathetic attempt and the marmot mocked her, emitting another sharp trill.

On a ridgeline above, she caught sight of an enormous goat. Magnificent horns curved down over its back as it grazed peacefully. It raised its head and stared directly at Amika. She held her breath, heart pounding savagely, afraid to move. After a few moments, it ambled over the ridge in unhurried complacency, looked at her over his shoulder, then it disappeared on the far side of the hill. Wonder paralyzed Amika. She could not wrench her eyes from the ridgeline. She hurried back to Ane's hut in awed silence.

"I saw the most wonderful vision," she blurted out breathlessly. Ane looked up from her baskets. "Today I climbed to a high ridge, higher than I've ever gone before. I saw a magnificent ram with horns so massive they curved down to the middle of its back."

Ane was instantly attentive. "Tell me everything." She seated herself on the low wooden stump she used as a chair. Sitting cross-legged at Ane's feet, Amika recounted every detail of the animal she had seen silhouetted against the corrugated clouds.

"Do you remember whose animal this is?" Ane quizzed her.

"It was no one's animal. It was as wild as the wind."

"In the stories I have told you," Ane prodded. "Who appears as a ram?"

"Mari?" Amika's voice quavered.

Ane rose and began pacing in circles. "Stand up, my girl."

Ane inspected Amika closely. Graceful curves had replaced Amika's angular limbs. Her face had narrowed and softened, and her abundant hair, the color of golden walnut, rippled in soft waves down her back. Somehow Ane had failed to notice ripening fruit hidden among the brambles of everyday life.

"Yes," Ane was decisive. "This was a sign from Mari. It is time for you to be introduced to the others."

"Which others? Who are you talking about?"

"A few people like us remain, scattered through the forests and hills. We are keepers of the Old Ways. We meet during the summer solstice. I have not gone to the gathering for many years. It is a long trek through rugged country, but this year we must go. They will be most interested in what you have to say."

When the days stretched out in long, languid leisure and the nights graciously made themselves small, Amika and Ane set out to the northern sea to join the gathering of the Wise Women. They trudged for three days over steep, rocky hills and through lavish and green pastures, making rough nightly camps.

Ane's brisk walk belied her age as they ambled over sinuous, well-trodden paths used by local people and their flocks. They slept rough, wrapped in their cloaks huddling around a small fire. Though her body begged for rejuvenating rest, Amika could not sleep. Anxiety gripped her by the throat as if physically choking her. Sleeping in the wild did not trouble her, nor did she fear danger. Rather, she felt as if she was crossing a great crevasse separating her old life before her mother was dragged away from a new and alien future. As she watched the coals cooling in their small campfire, two bright tears squeezed from Amika's eyes. She breathed in the scent of her threadbare woolen cloak, savoring its familiar smell. Its embrace physically tethered her to the past—winters before the hearth, summers roaming the hillsides at her mother's side, the last remnants of her past life.

By the second day, Ane's energy flagged, and she stumbled as the trail grew rockier. She leaned heavily on her walking stick, the one she had embellished with carved images of sun and moon. Late in the afternoon, their shadows lengthened in the slanting rays of the sun that perched precariously for a moment at the top of a distant peak, then sank heavily, like a stone thrown into a pond. That evening they camped at the edge of a dense forest where the land began to rise to meet the mountains.

"Amika, my girl, please go see what you can find for our dinner. I still have a bit of cheese and a few potatoes, but we will need more. Tomorrow we turn northward toward the sea."

Amika considered the view to the north. Ane was right. They would need a hearty meal if they hoped to have enough energy to scale the craggy mountains separating them from the northern sea. She wondered how Ane would endure the strenuous hike.

"What are you waiting for?" Ane scolded. "Though the view is new to you, I'm sure you've noticed that the plants are as familiar as my face."

Amika did not need to search long. The remoteness of the area protected the plants from gleaners like herself, so she had a lush banquet from which to choose. Rustling through the bushes, she discovered blackberries among the brambles, pulled up chives from among the grasses, and cut wild asparagus slightly past its season but still tender. She even found watercress in a shallow, sweet-water pond. By the time she returned to their campsite, kindling was already turning to coals in the shallow fire pit Ane had hollowed out. Water simmered in the ceramic bowl Ane had tucked into the sack she carried slung over her shoulder. Amika added the plants to Ane's diminutive potatoes, now swimming in the hot water.

The two women, one young and one old, each buried in her own thoughts, settled themselves around the fire to absorb its scant heat. Night-blooming flowers—primrose, campion, and nightshade—scented the cool air. Their white flowers glowed in the soft, waning light, attracting moths that buried their faces in pollen-laced blossoms.

That night, exhaustion seduced Amika into sleep. In her dreams, she saw men playing tug-of-war as they had on Saint Fermin's Day in the village. But they did not pull on a rope. Each team gripped the edge of her woolen cloak. Back and forth they yanked against each other until they tore it in two. Blood seeped from its ripped edges. Amika awoke horrified, her heart pounding and her face awash with tears. She peered into the sky. In the nebulous face of the moon, she recognized the face of Mari smiling down on her.

Amika fingered the braided hair necklace her mother had given her when she was a little girl and prayed to her mother's spirit.

"Mother, keep me safe as I follow Ane to a place I've never imagined," she whispered. *"She tells me it's full of wonders, but I don't want to lose you or the mysteries and miracles you taught me. I feel like the child brought before Solomon, claimed by two mothers, in danger of being cleaved in two."* The prayer relaxed her, and the jealous arms of sleep reclaimed her.

The next day, the trail turned abruptly north. By midday, they came face-to-face with the high peaks of the Cantabrian Mountains. Great pillars of rock jutted abruptly upward, narrowing their view of the sky to a thin corridor of cloud-pocked blue. Ane's pace slowed as she toiled up the steep slopes toward the pass. Torrential rivers hurtled through deep valleys. Pastureland disappeared, displaced by lush forests. A dizzying variety of leafy deciduous trees elbowed each other for space on the rocky outcrops. Ash, linden, bay laurel, maple, oak, and birch clung to the mountainsides like ivy.

On their final day, they gained elevation. Lush meadows carved out small places for themselves among thinning forests. They paused on a ridge between two steep valleys for a midday meal of cooked potatoes and onions. Diaphanous, misty clouds swelled up from the valleys below, bringing with them a faint whiff of sea air. Dirty snowbanks huddled against the north sides of trees. Griffon vultures floated on the updrafts, drawing lazy loops in the sky. A snow finch flitting from branch to branch above them scolded with its piercing, shrill "pee-pee-pid-eee, pee-pee-pid-eee" call.

As they rose to go, an enormous goat with horns curving dramatically over its back sauntered across the path before them. It stopped and looked straight at them before disappearing into the thick foliage. Amika and Ane looked at each other, completely awed by the Ibex.

41

"He came for you, Amika. He is meant to bless your trip to the sacred caves."

Amika stood awestruck, unable to respond. She was beyond speech. She could hardly argue that this was not a powerful sign that she was on the right path. It seemed obvious that the ram was a portent intended for her alone. They continued in silence over ridges, through valleys whose vertical walls towered over them, toward the sea. That night they sat close to each other in front of their campfire. Ane reached out and wordlessly took Amika's hand in hers and pressed it against her heart.

"You are the child of my heart, dear girl. We were meant to find each other."

Cold mountain air hurried them on their way the next day. Mossy, green-haired cliffs dropped down to a pristine, white sand beach. Amika and Ane veered off the established trail to descend an inconspicuous track to the beach. As they approached the sea, the low arch of a cave entrance emerged from the dense foliage. Smoke rose into the humid air from dozens of small fires scattered through the woods, making the place resemble an encampment of gnomes. Women of every description—girls and crones, elegant and tattered, squatty, and stately—tended their fires. Fecund forest air hummed with hushed conversations. Ane ignored all of them and walked to the cave entrance. The mouth of the cavern was guarded by a tall, willowy woman of indeterminate age wearing a seamless white tunic. A red scapular like a table runner hung down in front and in the back with only a hole for her head. The sleeveless garment gave her the appearance of a monastery nun.

She smiled. "Sister Ane, how nice to see you again. It has been many years. Who do we have here?" She shifted her smoky gray eyes to Amika.

"Greetings to you, Zavia. This is Amika, my apprentice." Amika swiveled her head toward Ane.

Is that what I am now? Your apprentice? Amika wondered.

"She recently experienced a visitation from Mari in the guise of a mountain ram, no, two visitations. The second one was just last evening. He came so close we could have reached out and touched him. He looked directly into Amika's eyes." Ane's measured tone belied the wondrous rarity of such a vision.

"Ah well, Amika." She folded Amika's hand into her own long-fingered grasp, creating a cool clamshell. Her eyes settled on Amika's face. "That is a very powerful omen, indeed. Mari has shown herself to you, a rare blessing. I understand this is your first visit to the cave of the Ancient Ones." Releasing Ane's hand, Zavia settled her gentle palm on Amika's head. "You are welcome among us."

"How are the others? Did everyone arrive safely?" Ane reclaimed the woman's attention. "What news is there? Are they all keeping safe?"

"The news is not good, Ane. Trouble has been stalking many of our friends. Religious witch hunters have been searching everywhere, hauling off any of the Wise Women they find. I'm sure you know the fate that awaits them." Her eyes flashed.

"Pogroms are being waged against us near our own woodlands," Ane admitted. Amika and Ane exchanged an eloquent look. "I am hidden as far away from other people as I can get. I seldom see others." Ane's brightness began to fade.

"What about the girl? How did she come to you? Is anyone looking for her?" Zavia asked sharply.

Ane was uncharacteristically evasive. "Her family is dead. She was quite lost and near starvation when Mari brought me to her." Ane's gnarled hands rested on the head of her walking stick as she hunched over. "I want to show the girl the cave before the ceremonies begin," she said, hoping to divert the conversation away from the dangerous precipice of fear.

Zavia angled slightly to the side and swept her arm toward the cave's entrance, smiling as Ane and Amika stepped into its depths. They walked in silence for a short distance, stopping before the cave, its darkness entirely swallowing the bright light of day. Amika peered into the depths until her eyes adjusted. The walls of the cave leaped to life. Beautiful bulls painted with red ochre and outlined in black kohl stared at them. She recognized many of the animals depicted on the cave walls—a large doe, two squat horses, a wild boar. But others were a complete mystery to her.

"You do not recognize some of these animals," Ane explained as if reading her mind. "They existed in the distant past among the Old Ones who lived at the foot of the ice mountains before they melted into memory. These animals were sacred to them. We are here to reenact their rituals and prayers, and to honor their powerful spirits." Ane sighed. "The sisterhood shares the ages-old awareness that these creatures represent the gods who rule these caves."

Ane paused, allowing the raw beauty of this place and its mysteries to seep into Amika's soul. Then Ane led her a short distance further into the depths. She steered Amika into a side tunnel and gestured toward the low ceiling. Ghostly hands outlined by spattered halos crawled across the ceiling. *Ane was right. I could never have imagined this place of wonders.* Amika marveled. *These are the handprints of the people who created the paintings.* She lifted her hand and gingerly placed it on top of one of the ghost hands. It fit perfectly. A jolt of mysterious energy shot through her. *Their spirits are still here. I am standing in their footsteps, touching the same stone walls they touched. I can feel them.*

In her dreams that night, Amika ambled through a verdant landscape surrounded by huge red bulls with short horns, shaggy heads, and great, humped shoulders, like the ones painted on the cave walls. In her dream, she followed these animals to the mouth of another, larger cave. Before its entrance stood a beautiful woman in a brilliant red robe next to a huge ram with long curving horns like the one Amika had spied on the ridgeline.

The ram spoke. "You are welcome here among us, daughter. I will protect you from those who hunt you. My messenger, the red fox pup, told me your heart was open and you could grow to be a wWse Woman."

"The fox pup." Amika bolted upright from her pallet. *I have not thought of the encounter with the pup for a long time. Was it a messenger I was too ignorant to recognize?*

Throughout the following days and nights, the women of the forest greeted old friends, locked arms, and danced in circles around their cheery fires. Soon great caldrons of water boiled over open fires into which they sprinkled healing herbs, vervain, yarrow, fern, and mugwort, all at their most potent midsummer peaks, gathered from the nearby forest and glades. Some wore conical ceremonial headdresses or flower crowns, and fern garlands. The rocky beach resonated with their joyful celebrations. But their joy was tainted by fear. All was not well. Danger lurked in every sector. They exchanged chilling stories of witch-hunters, of women being dragged off to dungeons, and of burnings.

On the last day, Amika and some of the younger women climbed the nearby slopes with instructions that each of them should bring back the largest downed timber they could find. They scattered across the lower hillsides, calling back and forth to each other whenever they discovered dried logs to drag back to camp, where they deposited them on the beach. Tired and dirty from the work, a tall, lissome young woman with coppery tresses lifted her tunic and translucent under shift over her head and waded into the waves. The others looked at each other and within moments the beach was littered with their clothing. They played in the waves, splashing and laughing until their worries dissolved in the surf.

"Amika, the elders have decided to make you the torch-bearer for our ceremony," Ane informed Amika when they huddled around their fire that evening.

"But why me? You or one of the other elders should lead the ceremony," she objected. "I don't even know what the ceremony is, how can I lead it?"

Ane smiled and touched Amika's arm. "You have been chosen to lead this ancient ceremony in order to honor your encounter with the ibex, Mari's emissary. Tonight's rite honors Ortzi, the sun god whose gracious light warms our days. We meet during the longest days when Ortzi, the giver of life, is in his full glory, generously bestowing his favor on all growing things of this earth. You need not worry; I will walk in front of you. Just follow me and mimic what I do. It's a simple ceremony, signifying the moment of balance between the waxing and waning of the light."

As the evening sun kissed the gently lapping waves, they gathered on the beach. The elders directed the young women to stack the logs they had gathered into a conical shape around a pile of kindling. The tops of the dry logs leaned against each other conspiratorially. Zavia called the women to gather around her. Her dark hair tumbled down her back. An unadorned diaphanous white shift hung loosely around her. Apart from where the thin cloth rested on her shoulders, nothing touched her skin, not even a belt constricted the flowing garment.

"Tonight, we reenact the ageless solstice ritual. We give thanks to the pantheon of gods who maintain the balance of the world and help us live in harmony with the cycles of the earth. We are here to strengthen and nourish the bond we were given at birth with the great parent who sustains us all." She leveled her eyes at Amika and beckoned her with the flick of an upturned palm. She placed a torch in her right hand.

"Follow Ane, the wisest of us all."

Zavia struck the fire-making flint three times. The sparks landed on the oily torch. It flared to life, dancing and shifting in the night air. In a single file, the women followed Amika's torch in a large circle that spiraled in on itself, making a tighter and tighter circle. When she could not go further Amika stood at the center of a spiral of Wise Women. Ane turned to face Amika, who turned to face the woman behind her until all of them had turned. The outermost woman then led them in the opposite direction unreeling the spiral until they formed a great circle around the bonfire.

"Throw the torch," Ane whispered.

Amika did as she was told. In the next moment, the kindling's flames licked the dry logs until they were fully engulfed in an enormous conflagration. Zavia's high, clear voice rang out above the din of the fire. She intoned an ancient song sung by the Old Ones in a long-forgotten language. Amika stood transfixed. Ane reached for Amika's hand. Amika took the hand of her neighbor and so on down the line until all hands entwined. The fire threw quavering light and murky shadows on their faces. Out of the darkness another song arose, this one was a folk tune they all knew; it celebrated the long days of summer when love ruled the land and all creatures flourished. The women swayed and sang, their simple tunics lapping against their legs like the waves against the beach. As they left the circle, convinced that their way of life would be eternal, their hearts swelled, knowing they were keepers of their ancient traditions.

CHAPTER FIVE

Ane and Amika returned to their familiar forest. Another cycle of seasons came and went. Ane and Amika felt certain that their timeless way of life would endure forever. The memories of alarming rumors receded, softened by familiar routines, and then melted into complacency.

The illusion of security ended abruptly the following spring. Amika had been absorbed in gathering food and did not react to a twig snapping nearby. She did not raise her head when scuffling feet disturbed the forest's usual tranquility. She did not notice until a man coughed loudly as if to deliberately attract her attention.

Amika emitted a single shrill note like a bow being drawn across a violin string. Like a startled doe, she gawked wide-eyed and unmoving at the tall, slim man peering back at her. She stared for just long enough to register the bow standing in readiness at his side. Then she bounded into the shadowy forest. The bowman chased as Amika darted right, slipping behind a fat tree trunk, then left behind a hummock of ferns. Within a few minutes, he could see only leaves rustling as she disappeared. Still, the bowman pursued until he could neither see nor hear any suggestion that she had ever been there. Like an apparition, she had disappeared into the underbrush. Defeated, confused, and disoriented, the bowman turned and made his way back to his village.

"He will tell everyone. They will hunt us down! He will lead the mob to our hut." Amika's panicky words tumbled like pebbles in a torrent as she described the scene to Ane. Visions of her mother being dragged away knifed through her.

"You are probably right," Ane said in a less hysterical tone. "We must leave this place, but we will need a little time to plan." Her eyes darted to the baskets and bins lined up against the walls. "What will we take with us?"

"Where will we go?" Amika, still winded from her headlong sprint through the woods panted.

"We must find a more remote location. We need to sort through our belongings and pack only those items needed to start over in a new place." Ane rummaged urgently through baskets of food and bins of simple tools. They filled Ane's shoulder bag and a hastily improvised satchel made from Amika's wool cloak.

"Tomorrow we will rise with the sun and set off," Ane said.

"But where will we be going?"

"We'll take the trail toward the northern sea. I know a few others living along the way. We met some of them at the solstice celebration. They will help us." It was an urgent, haphazard plan, but it bolstered their courage knowing others would help them.

That night sleep was like a vapor, disappearing with the slightest movement. Amika and Ane laid on their straw pallets listening to each other's breathing, smelling the familiar fecundity of the forest, waiting for the morning light. But it was already too late. Danger stalked them even as they slept.

In the darkness, a cohort of woodsmen approached quietly. Unlike the rabble that had dragged away Amika's mother, these men were strong, well-armed, with bows, scythes, knives, and swords. When they tore open the door, Ane and Amika leaped to their feet, cowering and clinging to each other. Their traveling bags leaned against the wall of the hut.

"I see we have come just in time," the tall bowman declared. "The witches were prepared to flee. Search through every basket in this hut," he ordered. "I know we will find evidence of witchcraft."

The posse ripped open their bags. Finding little damning evidence in them, they pawed at the women's clothing. "Look here," a meaty lumberman said, lifting the pouch that hung on a rope belt around Amika's waist. He yanked the pouch from her belt, tore open the drawstring, and poured the contents on the ground. A few dried herbs, some tiny snail shells, a brilliant red wallcreeper feather, and a tuft of red fox fur tumbled to the floor.

"Quite a collection of tools for throwing hexes." He smiled, amused by the girl's fear.

"No!" She loosened her arms from around Ane and stepped forward. "Those are simply beautiful treasures I found in the forest. Nothing more."

"Is that right?" he sneered as he stepped toward her, looking down on her wide-eyed face. "We'll see what the jury has to say about that."

"And this one." Another man lifted Ane's thin arm. "Look! It's a devil's mark." The men drew close and examined a raised mole on her upper arm. "It's a witch's tit. The mark of Satan."

He dropped her arm as he would a rotten apple and smiled at the others. "We've done a fair night's work, boys. Now let's haul 'em in and collect our reward." They made jokes and sang raucous tavern songs as they dragged their witches away, yoked together by rope nooses that tightened if Amika or Ane struggled against them.

Ane's waist pouch containing her few precious keepsakes lay undiscovered under her tunic. It cradled two polished amulets—one the pearly white moonstone and the other the dark, stained hardwood four-leaf clover. Ane said a silent prayer the hidden icons would remain so.

"Where are we going?" Amika demanded.

"Listen to that one," the hunter laughed. "Isn't she the fearless vixen, speaking up so boldly."

He turned his leathery face toward her. "We're taking you to the village of Saint Fermin. They will decide what to do with you." The posse walked through the night, leaving Ane and Amika no chance to escape.

Amika's village lay nestled in the verdant valley just as she remembered it. Waves of emotion washed over her like a violent surf, leaving her gasping for breath. Nostalgia softened her heart. Fear hardened it. Anger burned her cheeks. Sadness drained them. The tiny village was too insignificant for either the Church or the Court of Navarre to maintain judges. Lacking any forethought beyond returning as conquering heroes, the captors had no other plan for bringing the captives to justice. They congregated in the plaza before the ancient church.

"Call the priest!" The tall bowman took charge, ordering the woodcutter to find the pastor.

The woodcutter banged at the rectory door with the butt of his axe. Father Ricardo emerged wrapped in a blanket, blades of bedstraw in his hair, sleep weighing down his eyelids.

"Who wakes me before dawn?" His high voice, sharp as vinegar, pierced the darkness. Amika stumbled when the bowman roughly pushed her forward "Oh, her!" he barked when he recognized Amika. "She returns. The devil's spawn."

"We caught them!" the bowman crowed. "Where do want us to put them?"

Father Ricardo hesitated as the gears of consciousness fully engaged. "We don't want them here. Things have changed. The bishop will no longer sanction a witch-burning without his approval. Lock them in the church basement. Tomorrow we will send them to Pamplona." He glared at Amika. One corner of his lip curled in self-satisfied antipathy, then slammed the door in her face.

Only one small, windowless chamber laid beneath the old church. When the church was built, it was meant for grain storage. It had not been used for decades. The bowman held the torch that lit up the cellar stairway as Father Ricardo rummaged through his ring of keys to unlock the door.

"Finally." His voice was unctuous and gloating. "Now you can join your mother." He snickered as he banged the door closed, plunging Ane and Amika into total darkness. They huddled in a corner, clutching each other through the long hours. Only the tolling of the church bells marked the passage of time.

At dawn, the captors dragged a farmer's hay wagon into the plaza, vertical posts protruded from a flat wooden bed. Before the church bells rang Matins, the time for morning prayers, Amika and

Ane, hungry and weak, were dragged from the basement and loaded into the wagon. Amika's woolen cloak caught on a loose hinge as they dragged her away.

"Stop! My cloak!" Amika grabbed the corner of her cloak as the hinge tore it from her body. "My cloak!" Amika wailed.

"Where you are going you will not need it. No one wants a cloak when standing at the gates of hell." The men laughed and made a merry show of tearing her cloak to shreds.

Venena Arrosa, Marco Mendoza, and a few others came to spit at them as they rolled out of the village toward Pamplona. Amika and Ane peered through the bars of their makeshift jail as the hay cart rattled through the street. Many villagers shrank back into dark doorways where they had hung mistletoe to ward off evil.

The caged women were nearly unrecognizable by the time they reached Pamplona. Hunger and worry had hollowed them out. Weakness crippled them. Their wagon rumbled through the four barrios of Pamplona—Basque, French, Jewish, and Mudejar Muslim. Each enclave crouched behind thick defensive walls like countries at war, each population profoundly antagonistic to the others. But none of them showed the least interest in the prisoners rolling past. If anyone noticed at all, they would have seen two women—a grizzled, wrinkled hag cradled in the arms of a sturdy, wide-eyed, wild-haired adolescent—sunk on their knees in a hay-strewn cart. The residents neither knew nor cared where they were going.

The cart rumbled to a halt in front of the Church of Saint Nicholas to unload its prisoners. Few people had ever seen the dank rock cubicles beneath the temple where they would be confined. The edifice was like nothing Amika and Ane had ever seen. Severe and nearly windowless, it loomed over the plaza. Vertical openings sliced through thick walls from which bowmen could rain arrows down on intruders. It resembled a fortress more than a church. Only its cross-shaped floor plan and a few stained-glass windows belied its religious purpose. The hundred-year-old church served as a seat of justice in this remote land far from papal authority.

Nothing in their experience could have prepared Amika and Ane for the tomb-like rock cubicle that awaited them. The walls were damp with beads of water that looked and smelled like sweat. A narrow wooden bench stood against one wall. Rat droppings peppered a floor strewn with rancid straw. Pallid light from the chamber's only window fell across a simple wooden cross nailed to the wall by a heavy spike. The window was situated high above their heads, puncturing the thick wall at street level. The fetid water that ran through the streets dripped through the window into their cell, feeding the gummy moss that clung to the walls. A mighty door with wide planks hewn from a giant chestnut tree and secured by a heavy iron lock slammed behind them with the finality of the last judgment.

"You should sleep here." Amika's arm around Ane's shoulders guided her to the only piece of furniture in the cell, a bench constructed from a single plank supported by two stout legs. "I can sleep on the floor." She looked doubtfully at the ground. "I'll clear a space. It will be enough." Her words were brave, but her stomach recoiled at the thought of lying down on the filth-encrusted floor and she bent in two and retched. Luckily, her stomach was empty, capable of regurgitating only a thin, yellow stream of bile.

Blustery spring winds blew through the small window. The chilly air against the seeping walls made their cell as frigid as a root cellar in winter. The stench of the bucket that served as their latrine penetrated their clothes, their hair, and every pore of their skin. Despite the dead weight of horror, the two women, weakened by hunger and exhausted from the long journey, finally slipped into a numbed sleep.

When they awoke, the withered light of early morning filtered through the grated window. Feet shuffling in the hallway woke them. A floor-level hatch in the thick door swung open and a disembodied hand pushed two heels of dry rye bread and two mugs of water through the narrow opening.

Amika jerked upright. "When will we be released? When will we have a trial? This is a mistake. I want to speak to the bishop," she demanded.

The tender, cracking voice of a youth shifting awkwardly between tenor and bass replied. "The bishop is not here."

Amika drew a breath sharp enough to impale a deer. "Where is he? When will he be back? You cannot just keep us here. I want to talk to someone in authority."

"That's not possible, and besides the bishop does not inform me of his travel plans, so how would I know?" Youthful annoyance tainted his words. He paused, but he did not shuffle away. "Maybe I can ask the bishop's Prior to hear your confessions." The hatch dropped closed abruptly, signaling the end of the conversation.

By the time the Prior finally visited on the third day, the dampness had turned each of Amika's wheezing breaths into a painful struggle. Ane's frail bones could be counted beneath her papery gray skin. Her scalp showed through her once-bountiful halo of white hair. It was an effort for her to open her eyes.

Both women roused from their stupor when the door cracked open just enough to admit a tall thin man wearing a long white robe. Over the robe, he wore a full-length cloak, every inch of which was intricately embroidered. He brought a whiff of fresh air in with him. The ponderous door resounded like thunder as it closed behind him. He turned to face Amika and Ane. His heart's cadence tripped. His stomach turned. Though the girl's moon face was haggard, he recognized the sturdy shoulders and the wide-set eyes. This was the daughter who fled into the forest when the village woman accused of witchcraft was dragged away. How long ago was that? Two, three years ago? He had been a newly consecrated Benedictine monk, visiting his mother in St. Fermin at the time. He remembered watching the woman he had known as a kindly healer being dragged to her doom. Though he knew she was innocent, he lacked the courage to speak up for her. He had done penance for this sin of omission, but the guilt he felt over his silence had never lifted.

How things had changed during that time. His star had risen from a scribe in the scriptorium to Prior, the deputy of the abbot. As his richly embroidered robe indicated, he now enjoyed an esteemed career amid comfortable surroundings. The girl's world had changed too. She had gone from little girl hiding behind her mother's skirts, to a witch's handmaiden, then to fugitive and prisoner.

Apparently, she had not lost her feisty spirit. The kitchen boy came to his door with the message that a woman in the dungeon demanded to see the bishop. It was outrageous, though a hint of admiration for her courage touched his heart. Despite her dire circumstances, she demonstrated the courage he had lacked.

Do I know you? Amika thought when the Prior entered their cell. *No, of course not. The Prior of the Bishop of Pamplona would never cross paths with an orphaned village girl.*

"I am Father Jeshua," he announced, evading Amika's eyes.

Still, she stared at him, rummaging through the detritus of her memories. "Yes! I do know you. You are from my village. You came to our door seeking help for your mother's illness when you were a young boy. My mother helped you." Amika's demeanor was direct and challenging.

"I am that boy," he admitted uncomfortably. "And now I am here to hear your confession."

"What do I have to confess? I am an orphan. This old woman saved me." She gestured toward Ane who lay semiconscious on the bench.

"Well that, you see, is the problem," the Prior explained. "She is known to practice witchcraft. Our watchers spotted both of you participating in the pagan rituals at the caves near the northern sea."

"You have spies?" Amika threw words like rocks aimed at his heart. "At the caves?"

"I wouldn't call her that. She was more than willing to offer her services. She has been valuable asset to the bishop, able to blend in. She did not have any trouble luring the younger women into the sin of immodesty, did she?"

The tall, willowy woman with the sheer slip under her tunic! The truth broke over Amika like the waves on that beach.

"Yes, the bishop stays very well informed about his flock." His voice was flat, betraying no emotion. "It is his job to defend the faith."

Amika ignored his comments. The bishop's world was as far from hers as the stars.

"She is a good, kind person. She saved me. She wouldn't hurt anyone." Amika gestured toward Ane.

"She may be a good person, but she is also a heretic. And so are you. Do you follow the Old Ways? Is that what she taught you during your time with her?"

His words were firm, but his heart wavered. Amika ignited an unfamiliar burning emotion in him, or maybe it was a yearning. But what did he have to yearn for? He had everything most men seek, with only one exception. Thus far in his career he had not wanted a wife and family. Yes, he sometimes looked at young women too long, and could not evade dreams of carnal love, he dismissed these as minor annoyances, something every priest sworn to celibacy experienced. With age and discipline such thoughts and urges subsided. He interrupted his chain of thoughts abruptly.

"I need time to think. I will be back." He turned and again slammed the great door behind him. Amika heard his footsteps retreating down the dark corridor.

Ane pushed herself into a sitting position with her wobbly arms. In a barely audible whisper, she spoke. "You need not tell him you know about the Old Ones. You can say they were only folk tales with no meaning."

"But I can't throw you to the wolves to save myself. I won't!" Amika sat next to Ane on the rock-hard bench, sheltering the old woman beneath her arm.

"I will die soon." Resignation verging on peace suffused her haggard face.

"No! You won't. I will take care of you. I'll give you my bread."

A wan smile cracked Ane's face into deep lines. "You can tell him you are a Christian. You must. You are a good girl, my daughter. It will be the truth if you tell him that part of you continued to cling to the religion of your mother. That is not a lie."

CHAPTER SIX

Amika lost track of time. One day blended into the next without end until one morning the jail keepers pounded on the door.

"Make yourself decent. You are going for a little ride. Just you. Not the old woman." Amika scurried to smooth her hair. She used her morning water to wash her face. It was the best she could do. The jailers led her away like an animal to the slaughter. A figure-eight of rope coiled around Amika's wrists and the now-familiar noose leash encircled her neck. Brassy sun beat on her shoulders. The smell of clean air, unfouled by subterranean vapors, flooded Amika's lungs, invigorating her like a mountain morning. Though she pinched her eyelids nearly closed, the searing light blinded her after the gloom of her cell. How long had it been since she and Ane had been imprisoned? She had tried to count the time as best she could, but the dim cell blurred the boundary between day and night. The angle of the intense sun confirmed her calculations that it must now be late summer. Once again, a patient mule hitched to a hay wagon pulled the girl through narrow streets to a dark alley. It stopped at a side door to the bishop's palace. The door led to a subterranean passageway far from the sumptuous main entrance with its curving twin stairways.

A guard manned the door. He nodded respectfully to Amika's captors then pushed it open, revealing a barrel-vaulted corridor. The searing sun disappeared, and she was swallowed by darkness once more, until they immerged from the corridor into a large chamber. It seemed cavernous to Amika after her cramped cell in the church basement. Ornate tapestries covered the wall behind a raised dais on which stood a long table that spanned the room from end to end. Upholstered, high-back chairs rubbed elbows behind the table. Amika's captors pushed her toward a short, three-legged stool that squatted before the table like a humble supplicant. There she waited, while she studied the room. Squares of wavy paned glass punctuated the massive stone walls. Everything about the room was austere except the indulgently carved chairs and intricately detailed tapestry.

Though Amika's education in Christianity was weak, she recognized scenes from the lives of the Savior and his mother, Mary. The rich colors fascinated her. In each corner of the tapestry was a square portraying a scene from the bible, each one illustrating a lesson for people who could neither read nor write. The central image showed the Holy Mother balancing the Christ Child on her knee. Amika marveled at the skill of the craftsmen whose individual stitches, so fine they were almost invisible, merged to create this convincing imitation of reality.

She was roused from her reverie by the sound of a door closing. Father Jeshua emerged from a portal behind the tapestry and took a chair, followed by a rotund figure whose abundant girth accentuated his lack of height. The heavy-set man took the center chair. Amika did not need to be told this was the bishop. A lustrous, embroidered green chasuble draped his sturdy body from neck to knee in graceful, voluminous folds. A tall, richly decorated, cylindrical hat perched on his head.

"Let us pray," the bishop intoned. His deep baritone belied his short stature. "Dear Lord, we pray that you bless us with wisdom in sentencing this wayward girl."

He has already pronounced me guilty. I am here to be sentenced. Amika thought. *I have not even had a chance to speak.*

He looked directly at Amika. In that moment she saw herself through his eyes, a dirty, disheveled wretch, in tattered clothes. Suddenly she was aware of the stench emanating from her unwashed body.

"The Bible says, 'you shall not suffer a witch to live.' That is why you are here." His face was soft and doughy, but his eyes were piercing black daggers. He looked world-weary but not hard-hearted. The bishop withdrew a handkerchief from his sleeve and brought it to his face. He inhaled the smell of sandalwood to ward off the miasma surrounding Amika.

"I am a Christian!" Amika wailed before he could pronounce sentence upon her. "You must let me explain."

A blankly curious smile curved his lips as if unsure whether he was amused or annoyed. "Is that right? I must listen to *you*? There is evidence against you." He hesitated. "If you are a Christian, as you say, you may prove it to me by reciting the Lord's Prayer." He leaned back against the cushioned seat, resting his laced fingers across his protruding belly and waited.

Amika's heart raced. "Our Father who art in heaven," she began. "Hallowed be thy name. Holy Mary Mother of God pray for us sinners." *What comes next? No, that was not right! I MUST remember.* Confusion engulfed her. She could not summon any more words. Snippets of phrases she could recall turned to soup in her muddled brain.

"I see," the bishop sighed in resignation. "I sentence you and your companion to burn at the stake for the crimes of witchcraft and heresy." He glanced down at the table, lost in his own thoughts. When he looked up again, he seemed surprised Amika was still before him. "Return her to her cell. Prior Jeshua, you can arrange the execution."

Father Jeshua stood and addressed the bishop directly. "I have known the prisoner since childhood. Her mother was a healer."

"There is no healing other than through God." The bishop threw him a dark look.

"She helped my mother," Father Jeshua continued, as if he had not heard the bishop's words. "I recommend she be sentenced to life in prison. She will not last long. Her companion is already at death's door. A prison death will not attract the attention of the king as a burning would."

Father Jeshua's words brought the bishop up short. He considered the situation. It was true that the king was trying hard to wrest power away from the church. He was limiting the role of ecclesiastical courts in favor of civil courts. But Father Jeshua's challenge was surprising. Any other man would have been shown the door, but Father Jeshua had an excellent mind, and his opinions bore the weight of intelligence. "You are right, Prior. I see the benefit of the course of action you recommend. Very logical, as always." Turning to the guards he waved his hand as if flicking away a fly. "Take her back to her cell." Amika was hauled by her leash back to her noxious hold.

That night Father Jeshua came to visit her. "I will hear your confession," he began unceremoniously. "I understand the twisted path you have traveled to reach this point. Until now you have been a victim of circumstance, innocent of intentional heresy." He scrutinized the ragged young woman before him. A flush of warmth rose to his cheeks. He looked quickly away. "Listen carefully. I am giving you an opportunity to redeem yourself and make a new start."

She stared at him with flat, uncomprehending eyes. She felt his heat. She was drawn to him as lightning is drawn to a tall tree. She allowed that force to pull her up from her abysmal despair into consciousness.

"Listen to me." He reached out and pinched her cheek as his mother had done when he was a distracted child, then held her chin firmly between his thumb and forefinger, forcing her to look only at him. "Tonight, I am going to loosen the grate on your window. You must climb out as quietly as you can, prop the grate back into place, and duck into the shadows. I will place scallop shells along the way out of town. From there, you will follow the shells that mark the Way of St. James. This gift comes from God, not from me, and He demands only one thing in return." Again, he searched her face for comprehension.

A flash of understanding glinted in Amika's eyes.

"Are trying to save me?" she asked, groggy and uncertain.

"Yes," he replied. "But you must promise me one thing. You will look for God's grace along the Way as you walk. If you walk with an open heart, He will find you." He reached out for her hand and turned her palm up. In it he placed four amber stones. "These stones symbolize lessons you need to learn. Right now, you are in the grasp of a false belief. I understand because I was raised as you were among people who have never fully accepted the good news of Christianity." He looked intently into her eyes, then quickly dropped his gaze, fearing he might drown their depths. "God is giving you this chance to see the true path. I do not know what form these lessons will take. By the end of your journey you will be transformed, no longer a lost soul suspended between the Old Ways and the true path."

Amika looked at the translucent amber stones in her palm. She picked one up and held it up to the dim light filtering in through the grate.

"You are saying that each stone represents a lesson I am meant to learn?"

"Yes. I dreamed about your mother," Father Jeshua's voice was clipped with urgency to make her understand. "I know she was executed unjustly. I stood by watching, knowing she was a healer, not a witch. You are a heathen, not a Christian, because of me. My inaction forced you into the arms of this pagan." He gestured dismissively toward Ane sleeping on the bench. "I am giving you a chance to redeem yourself. Just promise me you will do this. Follow the Camino de Santiago until you find an iron cross that sits atop a mound of pebbles. As you place each of these stones at the foot of the cross, you must give thanks for four lessons you have learned along the way. The lessons may come in many forms—people you meet, extraordinary events, serendipitous experiences. Be vigilant. By doing this you will understand how God's hand has guided you to the true faith, and you will willingly abandon the pagan religion. Just do this one thing, and you will be saved." His insistence drilled into her.

Amika stared at him, baffled.

"Do you promise?" He turned her face so she looked directly into his eyes. Again, a jolt through shot him. He brought her face so close their noses nearly touched. "Do you understand?"

"Yes, I see. By the time I reach the iron cross I will have learned four lessons. Then I will give thanks at the foot of the cross and I will be transformed." Amika repeated mechanically.

Father Jeshua released his grip on her chin. He dipped his thumb in a tiny vial of oil he drew from the pouch at his waist and traced the sign of the cross on her forehead. "Your sins are forgiven. As Jesus said to the woman at the well, 'Go forth and sin no more.'" He headed toward the door, but stopped, turned, and dropped the vial of oil into Amika's hand.

"This is holy oil, blessed last Easter by the bishop himself. You may need this so you can bestow blessings on others as I have done for you." With this he was gone.

She stared at the stones in her hand. Her heart fluttered like the wings of a captive bird against its cage. She felt as if she was standing at the edge of a precipice plunging into a new reality as blurred as a misty forest at dawn.

"You must go," Ane croaked. Ane, laying as still as death on the stone bench, had grasped the conversation's significance immediately. "He is giving you a chance to be saved, both physically and by his god."

"But I can't leave you here," Amika protested. "I don't need his god to save me."

Ane propped her frail body up on one elbow. "Listen to me. Mari brought you to me to teach you the Old Ways, and now she releases you. I release you. You must do this."

"But ..."

"No!" Ane mustered the last of her strength. "I have only a few more days to live. When I give my spirit permission to depart, I will be gone. I am prepared to die. You are not. I have heard of this iron cross sitting at the top of a hill made of pebbles. This place has been sacred to the ancient ones for all time, since before the Christians, since before the Romans, for as long as there have been people living here at the foot of the mountains. The Old Ones placed pebbles on this mound to request favors from the gods and to give thanks. How many pebbles do you think it takes to build a hill as tall as the building that now imprisons us?" She took a ragged breath. Her body sagged from the effort of talking. "That is how many hopes and dreams have been laid to rest there by the countless people who have placed their stones at this shrine."

Ane reached out for Amika's hand just as Father Jeshua had done. She pulled from her pouch the pearly stone with the serenely sleeping moon face, the memento of her dead baby, and tenderly placed it in Amika's upturned palm.

"I have protected this moonstone in my pouch since I buried my daughter. Now it is yours! Place this stone on the mound of pebbles at the foot of the iron cross, and you will put both our souls to rest."

Amika draped herself over Ane's fragile frame, nearly engulfing her. In that moment, she realized she had never once in all the time they had been together embraced Ane. She buried her face in the old woman's shoulder and wept. When she raised her head, Ane's shoulder was as damp as the walls of their sordid cell.

"How can I leave you?" Amika sobbed. "I will be a motherless child once again."

Ane held Amika out at arm's length and smiled weakly. "No, Amika, you are no longer a girl, no longer anyone's child. You are a young woman. Now leave!" Ane curled up on the cold stone floor, face turned to the wall, not wanting her teary eyes to betray her.

Late that evening, Amika muscled the bench to the wall under the grated window. It had rained earlier in the evening, making the streets as slick as slime. Amika pushed against the grate. She flinched when it clanged to the pavement. The noise seemed deafeningly. She waited. The silence returned. She knelt before Ane and embraced her with more tenderness than she had felt for anyone. She had loved her mother, but she cherished Ane. Ane's intense eyes glittered in the darkness.

"I can't leave you here," Amika breathed into Ane's silvery hair.

"My spirit is not within these walls. It never was. Do not worry for me. I will embark on my own journey before the morning light. My purpose here is done. I will be with you always. Now go." Ane gently pushed Amika away. "Go, I said!"

Amika stuffed the stones Father Jeshua had given her and Ane's amulet into her pouch and squeezed through the grate. She propped the grate back against the opening and turned her face toward the damp streets. Reflections of the glinting stars spangled the cobblestones with tiny points of light. At her feet lay a white conch shell, as Father Jeshua had promised. The crooked smile of the waning crescent moon lit Amika's way. She crouched low, slinking catlike around corners of buildings, keeping to the shadows, following Father Jeshua's path of shells.

CHAPTER SEVEN

Amika sat with her back pressed hard against the enormous stone blocks that formed the outer walls of the city. She was not alone. An assortment of men and women drowsed, waiting for the great doors to open at first light. A middle-age peasant snored, leaning against the wheel of his farm wagon. Strands of silver glistened in his thatch of black hair. His crossed arms created a bridge across his tented knees; and a worn woolen cloak sheltered his crumpled mass. Mounds of unsold produce moldered in the soggy hay of his wagon. A wine merchant was spending his night in slightly more comfort, sleeping on the rounded floor of a cart intended to cradle wine barrels. Tomorrow he would pull his empty cart back to Rioja, having nothing heavier to carry than a pouch full of gold coins. Amika fingered her braided hair necklace as she shivered, the last memento from her previous life, struggling to stifle her sobs.

"What is troubling you, dear girl? Now that you have woken me with your weeping, you might as well tell me," a disembodied contralto voice rumbled in the murky darkness.

Amika peered into the blackness, choking on her tears. An older woman wearing a simple, undyed robe with a belt of knotted rope, a cloak of the same undyed fabric, and a shoulder-length black veil slid closer. She scrutinized the sniveling, shivering almost-woman huddled against the ancient stones.

"Why, girl, you look like you haven't eaten in a week! Your skin is pale as parchment." Glossy chestnut eyes set in an honest, round face peered back at her.

"I am hungry. I'm cold." She stopped, suddenly realizing how childish she sounded. It was likely all the travelers were hungry and cold, sitting in the drizzle.

"But that's not why you're crying, is it?" the older woman continued.

"I've lost everything. I have nothing, no one. I see no hope for better things to come." *Why am I whining to a total stranger?* Amika asked herself. Every word from her lips revealed her to be a fool.

"You are traveling alone, then?" the kindly woman persisted.

Amika nodded. Her downcast eyes teared up again.

"Well then, you will walk with us," she declared matter-of-factly "We are a group of sisters making our way to our new chapter house in Estella, three day's walk from here. By the way, my name is Sister Lourdes. In my tongue it means flower."

Amika gazed at the self-assured woman with combined perplexity and relief. "My name is Amika. In my language it means beloved of God." Amika looked down the row of damp travelers lining the wall. "Where are the other sisters?"

"They will join us at first light tomorrow. They were sent to gather provisions for our new chapter house. Now, stop disturbing the sleep of your fellow travelers. Take this time to rest until sunup." The older woman leaned against the damp wall, pulled her cowl over her head, and closed her eyes.

When the slate sky lightened to a sad gray, a muscular, straight-backed man approached the gate. He planted his feet wide, pulled against a mighty winch attached to heavy chains and lowered the thick planks of the drawbridge until it thudded to the ground.

As if on cue, a covey of four nuns carrying baskets and bulging packs slung across their backs found Sister Lourdes.

"This is Amika," Sister Lourdes announced." I have taken her under my protection. She will walk with us to our chapter house in Estella."

The four sisters crowded around her, chattering like a covey of quail.

"Look at you! You're practically naked," one of them said, looking at Amika's tattered tunic. She put down her basket and rummaged around until she found a simple, undyed wool tunic like her own. "This, at least, will cover you." The sister was young, yet confident and self-assured. "Come with me." She took Amika's hand and led her to a small, recessed alcove in the wall. She brusquely lifted Amika's tattered, dirty smock off, and slipped the new one over her head. Amika closed her eyes, savoring the warmth of a dry tunic.

"Thank you," she sighed.

The young nun stepped back, placing a hand on Amika's thin shoulder and scrutinized the emaciated girl before her.

"There, now you look slightly less like a feral animal and more like a young woman. My name is Sister June," she replied. "And yours?"

"My name is Amika. Thank you for your kindness." Amika reached up and laid her own hand over Sister June's. With that gesture, Amika no longer felt completely alone.

The group of five sisters, with Amika in tow, crossed the drawbridge and set off on the three-day walk to Estella. The sisters spoke little as they walked, fingering their beads with cowls drawn over their heads against a cool drizzle. Just outside of town, they climbed a steep hill. At the top, they paused and looked back at the bustling city of Pamplona stirring to life below them. The descent was even steeper that the ascent. The drizzle made the damp rocks as slippery as wet soap. About halfway down the hill a tall, reedy sister, carrying a heavy basket secured by a forehead strap stumbled forward. Before the weight of the basket could pitch her head-long into the gravel, Amika stepped behind her, wrapped her arms around the woman's waist, and leaned backward until they both skidded to a stop.

"Thank you, sister." The lanky woman gulped great drafts of air, trying to calm herself, then turned to face Amika. She laid her open palm against Amika's forehead and traced a small sign of the cross with her thumb. "I bless you, child. Who are you? Are you one of us?" she asked, looking closely at Amika's undyed tunic. "I've never seen you before."

"I'm not one of those you call 'sister,' but my clothes were in tatters and Sister June gave me this tunic to wear."

"I see." The nun was spindly. Her squinty eyes, huddled too close together under a high forehead, barely making enough room for her long, thin nose. She examined Amika, unable to place her in any of the roles available to single young women. She was traveling alone, something no self-respecting husband would allow his wife to do, so she was not married. Her wild tangle of tresses was uncovered, eliminating the possibility that she was a young mistress of a good family. As their limited conversation had thus far revealed, her Ladino was rudimentary, and she had lapsed into the mysterious Basque language when at a loss for Ladino words, so it was likely she was uneducated. She was ragged and nearly naked when they found her at the city gate. Her heavily calloused feet revealed she had been a stranger to shoes for quite some time. The poor girl was obviously destitute. Despite her frailty, she was strong and nimble, exuding a strength that utterly defied her vulnerable appearance.

"You are a mystery to me, young lady, but I'm glad you are with us. You saved me from a bad fall on these slick stones. My name is Sister Caitlin. Come, walk with me."

Amika fell into step beside her. "Tell me, who are these women who call each other sisters? Your sister Lourdes said you were going to your chapter house. I have never heard that term. What is a chapter house?"

Caitlin suppressed a smile, not wanting to insult the girl. "I've never met anyone who didn't know what nuns are." Sister Caitlin looked at Amika quizzically. The girl did not appear to be simple-minded, but she knew so little of the world. She was as baffling as a river running uphill. "We are followers of Sister Clare of Assisi, the sister of Saint Francis. Surely you have heard of Francis of Assisi?" She paused. When Amika remained silent, Caitlin dropped the question and continued. "We are a group of sisters who live in community, away from the world. We are establishing a new house in Estella. There we will live a simple life of poverty and prayer."

"You have so many sisters. Do you have any brothers?" Amika asked.

Sister Caitlin's stern face melted like butter in a hot skillet. She laughed out loud. Amika glowered angrily and grew silent.

"I think you must have been living in isolation if you don't know what sisters are." Caitlin smiled at Amika's innocence. *This girl is almost as old as sister June, how could she know so little?* Caitlin thought.

"Yes, I have lived in the forest." Amika raised her chin in defiance. "And I have learned a lot. I could teach you things about which you have no knowledge at all." Her hissed words seeped out between clenched teeth. "Can you catch a rabbit with a string trap? Can you stay alive eating only wild-caught plants? Have you seen the caves … " She abruptly stopped her string of invectives. It was not safe to mention the ancient knowledge. Secret knowledge must be just that—secret.

"I'm sorry. I didn't mean to offend you." Caitlin reached for Amika's hand. "You're right. I know nothing of the knowledge you possess. Please forgive me." The fraught moment passed, and Sister Caitlin resumed her explanation.

"No, we sisters do not have the same mother or father," Caitlin continued. "But we do live together as a family. Sister Lourdes, the older woman you met at the city walls, came from a wealthy home. Her father had too many daughters and could not find husbands for them all, so he gave Lourdes to the Church."

"Gave her to the Church?"

"Well yes, in a manner of speaking. He sent her to be educated at the convent in Zaragosa, expecting that she would dedicate her life to the Church as a Franciscan nun. There she learned the religious principles of the Franciscan Order. Because her family was wealthy, and her father wanted her to be well educated, she learned all the skills necessary to administer the affairs of a community of nuns— how to manage money, how to make contracts with builders and tradesmen, how to care for the sick, and how to grow crops and raise animals so her community could be self-sustaining. Then he endowed her with a substantial estate. She is using the land and money she inherited to establish the new chapter house. That is why we are going to Estella."

"I think I understand. You are going to build a new village. But what is a chapter house?" Amika interrupted.

"Yes, we will be founders of a new community. But unlike other villages, ours will be dedicated to prayer and contemplation. Our chapter house will be a simple stone building with small sleeping cells for each of us. There will be a communal dining room, and a chapel where we will pray. Each of us has a special skill to support the good of the whole. We call sister Lourdes 'mother' because she is the head of our little family. She is generous and kind, but firm and strong-willed. She doesn't tolerate argument or disobedience."

Amika was thunderstruck. She barely understood what sister Caitlin was saying. She wanted to know more but did not want her ignorance to shame her again.

"What about the others? Did they also inherit wealth?"

"Oh no," Caitlin said. "Each of us has her own story. I can tell you mine, if you like."

"Yes, I would like that very much."

"My family was poor. My father was eager to have one less mouth to feed, so he married me off when I was younger than you are now." She paused, lowering her voice to a barely audible whisper. "This is a hard story for me to tell. No one except Mother Lourdes knows my history." She looked hard at Amika, wondering why she felt compelled to share her secrets with this strange girl.

"The man my father chose for me was a capable farmer with a fertile plot of land." She furrowed her brow. "But he was as mean as a snarling wolf." Caitlin held out her arm and pushed up the sleeve of her tunic. Her forearm was not quite straight. It had a hump at its midpoint. "See this? One afternoon a drenching rain forced him from his plot early. His newly scythed hay lay unprotected in the soggy fields. He was furious, thinking his crop would mold where it lay and a whole season's work would be wasted. He stomped in the door. I felt his burning anger the moment he walked into our cottage. I should have remained quiet, but I was young and inexperienced, so I told him he should leave his anger back on the sodden ground with his hay and not bring it into the house. He turned on me like a rabid dog and grabbed hold of my arm. I twisted away trying to escape. I heard a snap and pain blazed through my forearm. He held on and pulled my arm as hard as he could, until a ragged edge of bone poked through my skin. When he saw what he had done he stopped pulling and tried to staunch the bleeding. I wailed wildly all night long, like a woman in the throes of childbirth. In the morning, remorse overcame him, and he brought me to the convent hospital in Pamplona where the Franciscan sisters set and splinted my broken arm. When it healed, I went home to the man I married. He tried to be a good husband, but his remorse was not strong enough to slake his fiery rages. Again and again, he pounded bruises into my flesh and blackened my eyes. He was powerless against the howling demon of his anger, and for this I condemn him. But he also had a conscience that tormented him. Soon he could no longer face the damage he was doing to me. He started disappearing for days on end. Finally, I fled to the good sisters who had healed me at the convent hospital. He discovered where I had gone and hunted me. Mother Lourdes met him at the convent doors and stared him down, arms crossed over her chest. She would not yield to his bullying threats. She saved me. I have no doubt that he would eventually have killed me in one of his explosive rages."

"I'm glad you are free of him," Amika said. "I am seeking my freedom too."

Sister Caitlin considered attempting to ferret out an explanation from the girl, but Amika had withdrawn into a wounded silence that Caitlin sensed was too raw to disturb. Instead she explained the sisterhood, described their daily routines, and the cycle of prayers that governed their day at three-hour intervals beginning before dawn until sunset. It was enough for Caitlin to walk in silence by her side. It was enough for Amika to know that she was not alone.

For three days Amika walked with the sisters, enjoying their companionship and a sense of security she had not felt since she was a child in her mother's garden. Sometimes they chatted companionably. At other times, the sisters lost themselves in prayer. Amika found solace in the rhythm of footsteps crunching on the gritty trail, and the great green swaths of pastures and woodlands that blanketed the low hills. Peasants walked, traveling tradesmen drove donkey carts, and the occasional wealthy landowner trotted past on a richly caparisoned horse. No one took notice of a band of sisters except the devout peasants who stopped them to kiss the hems of their tunics, begging that the sisters pray for them. The sisters honored every plea for prayers, muttering over their rosary beads on behalf of each wandering soul who requested their intercession. Peaceful miles flowed beneath their feet as easily as water under a bridge, until they came to the widest river Amika had ever seen. A magnificent stone bridge spanned the waterway. Five graceful arches met their reflections on the tranquil river's surface, creating the illusion of perfect circles.

The serenity of their journey ended abruptly when they encountered a knot of ill-tempered townspeople encircling a sturdy young man trying to cross the bridge. They shoved him from one angry man to another, closing in on him like a pack of wolves on a deer. Despite his unkempt thicket of shaggy hair and his rumpled appearance, a finely embroidered, padded doublet hugged his well-muscled torso. He held himself erect like a patrician, trying to maintain his dignity. One of his tormentors reached out and grabbed his wrists, turning them over, gesticulating excitedly to the others.

"Thief!" the swarthy villager howled as he held the man's arms in the air. "See this? See his palms?" Curious onlookers clustered around. Angry, half-healed burns scarred his open palms.

Amika and the sisters joined the cluster of curiosity seekers. *Why are his hands burned?* Amika wondered. Her answer came with the accuser's next outburst.

"That is the mark of a thief!" he thundered. "When a man is caught stealing, he is publicly punished by holding a metal rod, heated in a blacksmith's forge, across his palms. These are the wages of sin! The pain of the punishment is small in comparison to the flames of hell." The roar swelled from the outraged throng.

"Thief!" The angry accuser bellowed above the crowd. "I felt someone trying to steal a loaf of bread from my satchel. I turned and caught him in the act. Look at his hands. This is not the first time he has stolen." He unsheathed his knife and sliced through the half-healed burns. A stream of crimson trickled from the gashes and splashed to the cobblestones. The angry accuser brought his face close to the thief's. "We don't want your kind in our town! Now go!"

Satisfied by his retribution he turned his back and led the rabble down the street, leaving the man to stand there, bleeding. Roars of outrage transformed into self-satisfied laughter as they lumbered toward the tavern to celebrate their righteous indignation.

The burned and bleeding man staggered down to the water's edge and plunged his hands into the river. Sister Lourdes did not hesitate. She slipped and skidded down the riverbank.

"Come, all of you!" she called to her small flock of sisters. They quickly gathered around. "Remember Jesus's words: 'whatever you do for the least of these, you do for me.' It is too bad Sister Aliza is not with us. She is blessed with healing skills."

Amika was the first to slither down to the riverbank. With the delicacy of a mother opening the fists of her newborn she pried the man's hands open and bathed them in the cool water. She pulled her pouch from beneath her tunic and withdrew the vial of oil Father Jeshua had given her.

"Don't worry," she consoled the man, "this oil will sooth your burns." She gently worked the oil into his palms. Without hesitation she tore a strip of linen from the hem of her tunic and bound his wounds. "My mother was a healer," she explained. "I have seen her apply animal fat to burns many times. This is holy oil. Your hands will mend."

She helped the man to his feet. They stood together on the bank with all eyes trained on them. They faced each other, momentarily lost in each other's eyes. Amika tore her gaze away and laughed. "Look at us," she said. "We look like a pair of muddy dogs."

"You will walk with us," Sister Lourdes declared. "No one will molest you if you are guarding a group of sisters." She thrust her heavy walking stick into his bandaged hand. It had knobby head that looked like a battle ax without spikes. "Make yourself useful. Try to look menacing, as if you are protecting us." She turned and struggled back up the muddy bank, but without her walking stick she slipped and slid. The thief came to her side and placed his forearm under her bent elbow. In the other hand he gingerly held the walking stick.

Now that calm was restored, the curious crowd dispersed. The impromptu company of strangers resumed their journey—five nuns, one wide-eyed young woman in a torn habit, and one wounded thief with the bearing of a king.

Amika made her way to the thief's side, struggling to keep pace with his long strides. She studied him as a scholar studies an obscure text. Though he was not inordinately tall, his regal bearing made it seem as if he was looking down from a great height on those around him. His black hair was matted and long. His padded doublet, which had once been of the highest quality was now dirty and frayed. But the rare luxuries of leather shoes and leggings aroused Amika's curiosity most of all. Was he a hunter? Or perhaps he was a knight back from the crusades? Or maybe he was a landless peasant who gleaned the leather clothes from a dead man he had robbed. Curiosity overcame her.

"What brought you here? You do not look like anyone else I have seen along the way. Where are you going?" Amika's inquisitiveness bubbled to the surface.

He looked at the girl's moon face and his heart softened. She reminded him of his younger sister in their days of innocence, before their lives were torn apart.

"I am walking the Way to the Cathedral de Compostela in Santiago," he replied.

"Why are you walking? Where are you from? Your clothes are different from any others I've seen." Her questions piled atop each other like puppies at play.

The man looked straight ahead, but try as he might, he could not suppress a smile. The girl's innocence was disarming. *How old was she?* he wondered. He stopped and looked directly at her. She was a walking contradiction. She wore the habit of a Franciscan sister, now muddy and torn, but she did not comport herself like a nun. Her strides were long and unladylike. Her calloused feet were bare. She flung her arms and legs forward like a gangly boy. Her genuine curiosity was uncensored by inhibition. She appeared undernourished, as if hunger had stunted her maturation. She was simultaneously guileless and unworldly, but with the haunted eyes of someone who had suffered. He guessed she was about fifteen years old, though she might be older had her figure been as well rounded as the wealthy heiresses he had known in a former life.

"I should ask you," he said. "Why are *you* walking? Are you really a nun? Are you going to Santiago de Compostela?"

Amika smiled coquettishly. "I asked you first. For now, I will tell you I am an orphan. My feet were set upon this path by others so that I might heal my soul and accept what they call 'the one true God.'" Her playful attitude dissipated like dew at sunrise. "Now you."

"If I am to tell you my story, you should know my name. I am Mateo Faniez, the famous stone carver of Jaen." Mateo extended one leg forward balancing his weight on his back leg, and bowed formally, sweeping the ground with a wide arcing gesture.

Amika giggled, not sure if he was mocking her or being serious.

"I grew up in a Jaen, a prosperous town in Andalusia. I came from a long line of famous stone carvers. Through many generations my family's beautiful stonework has adorned cathedrals, castles, and mosques. I recently worked on a royal palace called the Alhambra.

"My family was wealthy and enjoyed many privileges not often afforded the Christian minority in the Muslim town of Jaen. The Muslims treated us fairly and did not try to suppress our religion. Unfortunately, my town was mostly destroyed over the course of a terrible three-year battle. At first the Christian Castilians launched attacks against the city gates, but we resisted. For two years the King of Castile waged a relentless siege against us. We suffered terribly. To smuggle food into the city was to risk being run through by the guard's sword. No food reached us. Our water turned bad. Diseases laid the population to waste. I watched my family die one by one. My younger sister, who looked so much like you, was the last to die. Have you ever watched people you love die of starvation?" Mateo glanced at Amika.

Amika nodded. She understood starvation and empathized with his suffering.

"Four years ago, Muhammed, Jaen's Moorish governor, surrendered our city to the King of Castile in order to secure peace in Granada, his last stronghold. He sold us out to the Christians in return for peace for his capital city. Castilian troops moved in and took whatever they wanted. One of the things they wanted was our beautiful home. I had been living there alone, the last survivor of my proud family. What could I do? I am just one man." Mateo hung his head, shamed by his helplessness. "The conquering Christians took my inheritance and gave me a hovel in which to live. Every day I watched them coming and going from what had been my family's home for generations. Whereas Jews, Muslims, and Christians had previously lived in harmony, the Castilians behaved with haughty disrespect toward both Jews and Muslims."

Mateo heaved a deep sigh and continued. "One night I could stand it no longer. I climbed into the window of my former bed chamber to reclaim my weapons and a few cherished mementos. My home was well guarded, and the lookouts spotted me. They brought me before the magistrate and convicted me of theft. Theft!" Mateo shouted. "Is it theft to reclaim the medallion my mother had received as a wedding gift from her own mother?" His cheeks reddened with anger and humiliation. His breath came in deep gulps. "I guess I should be glad," he went on. "I was brought before the magistrate. He had known my well-respected family and was lenient. He sentenced me to suffer the ritual burning of my hands, traditional punishment for a thief. He returned the medallion to me. In a final gesture of mercy, he scribbled a message on a parchment page and handed it to me.

"This is your safe passage document. Protect it carefully. If you complete the pilgrimage to Santiago, go to the bishop's palace and show him this document. It will be proof you have completed your sentence and your conviction will be overturned."

"May I see your mother's medallion?" Amika was intrigued. Mateo withdrew it from his pouch. Amika staggered with shock. Without taking her eyes away from it, she fished her hand inside her own pouch and drew out the pendant Ane had given her. Side by side, on their two open palms were identical, moon-faced cameos. Mateo's was rimmed with finely wrought silver imbedded with precious stones. Amika's was unadorned. They looked at the ornaments then at each other, speechless in astonishment.

"How can this be? she said. "My second mother, Ane, gave this to me and instructed me to place it at the base of the Cruz de Ferro. Do you know the place?" Her hand dipped into the pouch again and came out with four amber stones. "As I lay moldering in my prison cell, the priest who freed me gave me these four stones and instructed me to place the stones at the foot of the cross as the price of my freedom. I also have a mission. The stones are meant to save my soul. The moon-faced stone honors a tradition much older than Christianity."

As disjointed as Amika's tale seemed to Mateo, and as other-worldly as Mateo's was to Amika, their wildly divergent paths had crossed here on the Camino de Santiago.

Mateo was fascinated, but before he could unearth any more details, Sister Lourdes's commanding voice broke the spell.

"That's quite enough of that! I told you to protect us, not weave tales for a girl's amusement. Now young man, please return to your duties or I will take my staff back from you and guard the sisters myself."

CHAPTER EIGHT

Brilliant olive, grape, and apricot orchards dotted the rolling hills. Gauzy veils of scattered clouds trailed across the sky. Fog no longer dimmed the morning hours. Rather, the daylight broke with crystalline clarity. The air smelled sincere and safe. The earnest green of the fields reminded Amika of her mother's garden after a rain.

On the third day the travelers stopped on the hilltop overlooking Estella, a handsome city straddling the Agra river. It exuded a self-satisfied pride. It was proud of its palaces, stately homes, churches, convents, bridges, and beautiful buildings, all displaying the city's emblematic eight-pointed star.

Sister Lourdes approached Amika and drew her aside. "Now you must decide your next steps," she began. "You are welcome to join us. You are a strong young woman. Judging by your handling of this young man's injuries I suspect you know something about the healing arts. If you know your way around a kitchen garden as well, you could be a great help to our new community."

Amika's shoulders slumped. She was torn. These caring women had taken her in, clothed, fed, and cared for her in her most desperate moment. They could fill the aching void left by the family she had lost. She knew eventually they would want her to join their spiritual community as well. Amika could not picture herself rising at five in the morning to pray in a dark, damp chapel. Nor could she tolerate the regimentation of a religious life.

"I'm sorry, sister. You never pressured me to tell my story, and I appreciated that immensely. But I am running from Pamplona because I escaped from jail."

Sister Lourdes drew a sharp breath despite herself. "What did you do? Why were you in jail?"

"I was on trial for witchcraft." Sister Lourdes involuntarily clutched the crucifix that hung around her neck. "I am not a witch. Neither was my mother, but jealous neighbors accused her, and she was burned at the stake." Amika saw shock crack Sister Lourdes's normally calm expression. Amika forged on. "I survived in the forest with the help of a good woman who cared for me and nurtured me as if I were her daughter. She lived according to the Old Ways of the ancient people who lived here long before the birth of Christianity. The Christians call them pagans or witches. I call them Wise Women. We were hunted down and imprisoned. A good Christian priest arranged my escape and gave me a mission to fulfill. I cannot stop before I fulfill the promise I made to him and to the generous soul who was a second mother to me."

A long sigh hissed from Sister Lourdes's lips. She shook her head from side to side.

"I will never forget you." Unapologetically Amika faced Sister Lourdes. "You treated me with kindness and accepted me without question despite my wild appearance and demeanor. You never asked for an explanation of my desperate situation." Sister Lourdes saw her reflection in Amika's moist eyes. "You are a true Christian, as Jesus meant his followers to be."

"Nor will I forget you," Sister Lourdes replied. "You will always have a home among us if you choose to return." With that, she laid a palm against Amika's forehead and traced the sign of the cross. "Go with God."

One by one the five sisters embraced Amika and turned to follow their Mother Superior into the handsome town shining on the banks of the beautiful river. Mateo returned Sister Lourdes walking stick to her. Then he and Amika walked together toward the town.

The town was divided, as Pamplona had been, into three separate, walled districts, the Frankish, Jewish, and Muslim neighborhoods. Amika and Mateo made their way through the narrow streets of the Christian barrio to the ancient monastery of Irache, where he knew they would find shelter with the Benedictine monks. That evening a dozen pilgrims ate in silence seated at long tables in a long, narrow room with ribbed arches supporting twenty-foot ceilings. The unheated room was solemn as the monks chanted Vespers, the evening prayer. They ate their simple dinner of bread, cheese, and bone broth. When it was done, Mateo and Amika followed a scuffling, hunch-backed monk down the long corridor to their austere cells. A single candle shed wobbly light on the stone walls as their shadows wavered like black ghosts. Wordlessly the monk closed Amika's heavy wooden door, throwing her cell into blackness. Panic overwhelmed her. She could not catch her breath, and her skin erupted in a cold sweat. A weight as heavy as a blacksmith's anvil pressed down on her chest. The sense of confinement inside the clammy walls mimicked what she had experienced in the prison she had so recently escaped.

Through the grated window the face of the moon smiled down on her. She reached inside her pouch and cradled Ane's moon-faced stone in her hand until her heart stopped racing. She curled up on her straw pallet on the floor until her eyes drooped and sleep claimed her.

In the morning they ate in silence, seated alongside black-robed monks as they had the previous night. At first light the cloister doors opened. The pilgrims turned their faces to the west and set out walking through shimmering drops of dew.

"Were those men priests?" Amika asked Mateo as they walked away from the monastery.

"No, they are not priests. They are monks. They have dedicated their lives to God. They have vowed to live a simple life of poverty and prayer. They are brothers in the same way Mother Superior Lourdes and her nuns are sisters." He looked at Amika, wondering again about her age. Once more his heart softened as he looked at her quizzically upturned face. He wanted to protect her, but there was more to it than that. He wanted to be close to her. Abruptly he looked away. He stiffened. There was no room in his life for a soft heart.

The sparkling river slipped into and out of view as the Way meandered west. Hills capped with oak, beech and pine alternated with valleys thick with juniper, rosemary, and thyme. Flocks of sheep and cattle dotted lush hillsides. Along the river, narrow poplars ranked themselves in orderly rows like upward pointing spears of palace guards at attention. Vast vineyards stretched to the horizon.

As they approached Burgos, merchants of all kinds crowded the path. Donkey carts hauled flour to the mill and wine to the shops. Farmers herded cattle and sheep to the butcher. A dozen Templars on elegant horses muscled their way through the busy clamor of the crowd. Clad in chain mail and metal helmets, draped shoulder to knee in white tunics emblazoned with a red cross, they pushed people into muddy kitchen gardens and up against mossy walls lining the street, clearing a path through the crowd like Moses parting the Red Sea. A donkey reared, kicking an old man who crumpled to the ground. A mother tripped and landed on her knees, one arm breaking her fall on the rough cobbles, the other gripping her infant against her chest. Amika grabbed the woman's elbow and pulled her upright. Dazed, they pressed their backs against the wall. Having cleared the way, the Templars flanked a well-dressed man sitting erect on an exquisitely hand-tooled leather saddle. His long-legged horse, its coat lustrous and its hooves polished and glistening, strode past.

The cavalcade paraded past them, barely noticing the peons clamoring to clear the way. Amika had never seen a person so richly attired. His flowing robe had large sleeves embroidered with green, orange, and rose silk thread. An intricately wound turban encircled his head. She gawked at him until Mateo tugged her arm, drawing her attention away from the spectacle.

"Don't you know it's not polite to stare at people? Least of all at important people!"

"Is he important?"

"Have you no eyes? Of course he is important. His saddle alone is worth a fortune. And he carries important documents."

"How do you know that?"

"Look! His saddle bags are bulging with scrolls."

Amika focused on the saddle bags. The flap covering one of the bags hung loose and rolls of parchment peeked out over the edge, revealing mysterious letters like writhing snakes.

"What do the scrolls say?"

"Who knows? Maybe they are government messages, or battle plans, or a list of the king's debtors."

"I have seen written words in the prayer books when I was young," said Amika. "But none had strange letters like those."

"Yes, that is the Andalusian script of the Muslims. This is the script used in my home city, Jaen."

She resumed staring at the elegant horse and rider receding down the street. The cavalcade eased its way through the narrow lane, crowded on all sides by people and animals trying to move aside. But as the stately horse and opulent rider turned a sharp corner the unfastened saddle bag scraped against a stone wall, dislodging one of the scrolls. A parchment tumbled to the ground, unnoticed by the rider. It seemed no one else had noticed either. The people returned to the pursuit of their daily duties. Amika focused on the rolled parchment splayed on the dirty streets. She elbowed her way through the crowd, snatched it up and ran to catch the receding horse and rider. Mateo snaked through the crowd, trying not to lose sight of her and found her standing on the corner, parchment in hand.

"We must find him," Mateo said. "It would look bad if the authorities found us with this. They would think we were spies or simply thieves. Either way, they would not waste their mercy on vermin like us."

The two of them jostled through the narrow street, struggling to keep sight of the rider as he rounded a corner onto a wider cobbled avenue leading toward the city center. In this quarter of the city an assortment of tanneries, goldsmiths, and tailors lined the streets. They followed the horse and rider up a steep hill, finally catching up with him at the wall surrounding the Jewish quarter. Breathless and sweating, Mateo approached the horseman. As he had done with Amika, Mateo executed an elegant formal bow. The man looked down on him from horseback, puzzled by the incongruity of the grand gesture, perfectly executed by this disheveled man. He halted his horse and chuckled indulgently at the man's boldness. "Hold!" he called to his entourage.

"Sir," Mateo began. "You dropped this. It tumbled out of your saddle pack when you turned the corner and grazed the wall." He reached up, proffering the parchment.

"I saw it fall. I picked it up and we ran after you," Amika blurted out. The rider turned toward her, a young woman in a frayed nun's tunic.

The rider leaned down from his horse to accept the document, never taking his eyes off the pair. "Follow me," he said. "I want to talk to you."

Mateo and Amika exchanged fearful glances. "We didn't steal it. I swear," Mateo pleaded.

"Wait here," he ordered his retinue of Templars. "I want to talk to these two."

"I didn't accuse you. I just want to talk to you," he said, turning his attention back to the pair of misfits. His mild tone was reassuring. He led them to a covered portico in St. Martín's Square, where he dismounted. "Here we can have a little privacy. Tell me, who are you?" His piercing eyes, dark as mother earth, riveted them to the spot.

"I'm no one," Mateo answered. "Or rather, I used to be someone, but everything I once owned has been taken from me. Now I am nothing."

"And you, girl, where are you from? Are you a Franciscan nun?"

Amika watched his eyes wander over her tattered habit. "I am also no one. I am an orphan. Like Mateo, I have nothing and no one."

"There must be more to your stories than that. Come now, humor an old man."

"No!" Amika declared with a boldness that stunned both men. "My story is of no interest to you."

"Oh, but it is." A wry smile teased the corners of his mouth. "It's not often I meet an honest Christian."

"No," Amika repeated, less forcefully yet still adamant. The man was less amused now.

"Let us strike a bargain, then. You will come to the home of my cousin, who lives in this city. Since you are with me, he will show you the utmost courtesy and hospitality. Then you will tell me your story."

"Well," Amika cocked her head, torn between fear and fascination. "All right then, we will tell you our stories, but only if you will tell us yours." More serious now, she continued in a conciliatory tone. "I have never met a man like you, and it would be an honor if you would share your story with me. With us," she added with a sidelong glance toward Mateo, who stood thunderstruck by Amika's audacity.

"Spoken like a good negotiator," the horseman conceded. "I am Samuel Cohen. Now follow me." He remounted and gently nudged his horse forward through the streets until they came to an arched gateway. A heavy metal door inlaid with a pale quartz menorah topped by enigmatic lettering swung open and they entered the mysterious world of the Jewish quarter.

The elegant gentleman turned to address the captain of his Templar guardians. "You are dismissed. You can see my bursar for recompense for your services."

CHAPTER NINE

If the streets of the town had been narrow and winding, the streets of the Jewish quarter were downright serpentine, curving and recurving, crossing each other at peculiar angles. The buildings molded themselves into strange shapes to occupy every sliver of space. Samuel negotiated the labyrinth expertly. Amika and Mateo marched briskly behind, so as not to lose sight of him. He pulled his horse to a stop in front of a building whose blank façade divulged no hint of what it concealed. He pulled a thick cord, and muted bells echoed inside the walls. The door swung open, and a servant ushered them inside.

A shallow, rectangular pond shimmered in the center of a square courtyard. Unripe citrons dripped from branches competing for sunlight with sour green apples and persimmons. An elaborate colonnade of horseshoe-shaped Moorish arches shaded the walkway around the patio. The unfamiliar smells, the exotic architecture, the sunlight glinting off the placid blue pool absorbed Amika's senses. She felt as if she had been transported to another world, a foreign world unlike anything she had ever seen.

Two figures emerged from the shadowed arcade that ringed the courtyard. The man's robes billowed, while the woman's delicate silk mantle danced behind her as weightless as butterfly wings.

"Cousin!" Samuel spread his arms to embrace his kinsman. "*Aleikhem Shalom*. Thank you for welcoming us."

"*Barukh ha-ba*. Blessings on you," their host replied. "We received word you were traveling to Burgos and would be staying with us. We are honored by your visit."

"And who are these fellow travelers?" the lady asked, eyeing the bedraggled strangers.

"Let me introduce my traveling companions." Samuel extended his arm toward Mateo and Amika, who stood behind him, trying as best they could to appear respectable. "This is Mateo, and this young lady is Amika. They did me a great service today. Without their honesty my mission to Burgos would have been in vain."

As discreetly as she could, Amika brushed her knuckles against Mateo's, seeking the reassurance of his steady hand. A flash of warmth flickered between them. Though their eyes remained focused on their exotic hosts, an invisible energy leapt between them, binding them like barnacles to a barge.

"They have graciously offered to entertain us this evening," Samuel winked impishly at his cousin. "Aaron and Johanna, please forgive my presumptuousness in bringing these vagabonds into your home."

The breeze held its breath for a moment as Aaron and Johanna absorbed the sight of two unwashed peons in their sumptuous courtyard. In the next moment, their icy stares melted like frost on a sunny day. Johanna swept past Samuel. She laid one arm around Amika's shoulder in a silken embrace. "Well then, you are welcome in our house. I will wager you would love to see our hot baths. There is one for the men and a special one for us women. Let me show you the way." She smiled wryly over her shoulder at Samuel as she ushered Amika away.

"And you, Mateo." Aaron looked squarely at the swarthy man. "You could also use a good washing. And I will send my physician to look at the damage hidden beneath those filthy bandages," he said, pointing his chin toward Mateo's fists.

Mateo hardly recognized Amika when she and Johanna joined the family at the dinner table that evening. Her glossy burnt umber hair, half hidden by a scarf draped loosely over her head, shone as it tumbled down her back. Kohl ringed her wide-set eyes. Her oiled skin glowed and her cheeks and lips were tinted the color of redcurrant berries. The feral adolescent had disappeared, replaced by a lovely young woman. Mateo forgot to breathe as he gawked at her.

Aaron's three children entering the dining hall broke the spell. The little girl, whom Amika judged to be perhaps eight or nine years old, marched in with the officious demeanor of a big sister accustomed to exerting authority over her two younger brothers. She wore a simple floor-length tunic, and a transparent veil covering her fat nut-brown braids, the clothing of a miniature woman. Two boys straggled in behind her. Mateo and Amika exchanged incredulous glances. The boys were identical in age, appearance, and attire— knee-length undyed linen tunics cinched with colorful embroidered waistbands, and long black stockings. They took their places at the table, quieted, and folded their hands demurely in their laps.

"Benjamin, please recite the Brachot," Aaron directed one of the buys.

One of the twins, tall for his age but delicate, stood and recited. "He who brings forth bread from the ground. He who creates the fruit of the trees. Everything was created through His words. We are grateful to you, oh Lord, for thy bounty."

Figs, almonds, and olives crowded a plate at the head of the table where Aaron sat. In the center, steaming aromatic lentil stew rested on a trivet. Roast lamb with pomegranate sauce and dark rye bread, still warm from the oven, nearly made Amika swoon. A low rumble emanated from her stomach. Her eyes shot from face to face, fearful that someone had heard it, but no one even glanced up. When everyone had eaten their fill, Samuel called on Amika to relate her story.

"Amika," he began. "What an interesting name. Where are you from, my girl?"

Amika squirmed like a child. "I am from the land at the base of the Pyrenees. Our people have lived there for centuries, far from luxury and wealth."

"Ah" Samuel said. "So, you are Basque. That explains your unusual manner of speaking." Amika startled, unaware that even her speech marked her as different. "Now tell us your story, how did you come from such a distance to the kingdom of Castile?"

"I can't." Anxiety tightened her stomach and her meal threatened to rebel against her. Could this powerful, wealthy Jew turn her over to the authorities to be imprisoned once again? Amika met Samuel's gaze with an arresting boldness.

"Yes, child, you can. No one here will think badly of you," Samuel insisted. His tone was fatherly, but commanding, the voice of one whose authority is unquestioned. "I have seen much of the world's ways. But yours is a story I'm sure I have never heard."

Amika looked from one face to the next. All eyes rested on her in anticipation. None of those eyes reflected hostility or subterfuge. She relented and recited her tale—from her mother's fiery execution, to her rescue by Ane, her introduction to the Old Ways, her capture, imprisonment and escape.

Aaron and his family were captivated.

"We've heard there was still a race of people in the Pyrenees adhering to a primitive religion resisting Christianity. I thought it was only a rumor."

Shame reddened Amika's cheeks. "No! we are not primitive," she objected. "It is an ancient belief. It is old, but not primitive. The Old Ones respect the earth and all living and nonliving things upon it. They see the eternal in every blade of grass, hear the voice of the universe in every bird song. They honor the seen and unseen, the animate and inanimate forces that govern the universe. There is nothing primitive in that. There are not many people left who honor Old Ways. My second mother was a Wise Woman, and she was kinder than any Christian I have ever met. She taught me to live lightly upon the earth, gratefully accepting its gifts and wasting nothing. Without her I surely would have died."

"I meant no offence," Aaron continued. "I only meant to say how surprised I am to meet one such as you. I thought your kind had disappeared. What will you do now? You are yet young. Are you married to this man?" Samuel glanced at Mateo.

Amika blushed furiously. "No! I barely know him. I treated his wounds. Our paths crossed coincidentally. Serendipity threw us together."

Samuel raised his eyebrows. "You met simply by chance?"
"Yes."

"I wouldn't be so sure." His perpetual half-smile showed itself. "You know, some people believe that nothing happens by chance, that God knows our fates even before we are born. What happens was meant to be." In a more serious tone, he asked again, "Where are you going?"

"When I escaped prison, Ane gave me a memento to place at the foot of the Cruz de Ferro. Strangely, the good priest who freed me gave me four stones to deposit there also. I gave both of my rescuers my word that I would do this for them. I must fulfill the promises I made to the people who saved my life."

"Hmm, very interesting." Samuel said pensively. "And you, young man, what is your story? You don't look like a pilgrim."

Mateo recounted his story, adding details he had not told Amika, explaining that he was a dispossessed aristocrat. "I am Christian, a religious minority in my city of Jaen. Jaen is an ancient city. It had been a Muslim stronghold for hundreds of years, and the Moorish civilization dominated the city's culture and architecture. The Moors had a high regard for scholarship, and their madrassas offered the finest education available. It was well known that the Muslims excelled in learning. My father, wanting nothing but the best education for me sent me to one of the madrassas. My education included science, philosophy, and reasoning. I studied classical Greek and Roman knowledge."

"But I see you the bear the scars of a thief," Samuel said, glancing at his hands. The squalid bandages had been removed, the wounds treated with ointment and exposed to the air to dry and heal. "Would you care to explain that part of your story?"

91

Mateo bristled defensively. "I am not a thief, merely unfairly accused. I returned to my own home to retrieve a few personal items. But my home was no longer my own, having been confiscated by Christian invaders. I could have been hanged, but because of my family's centuries-old connections, I was sentenced to walk the Camino de Santiago as penance. I must do this to redeem my good name."

Samuel considered these two unlikely pilgrims thoughtfully. Both had warrior's hearts and would not likely allow circumstances to defeat them. "I wish both of you well and hope you accomplish your purposes. Thank you for sharing your stories with us, strangers as we are."

"Now it's your turn," Amika spoke up, prompting Samuel. "You promised."

Samuel smiled. This girl was indeed fearless, unintimidated by those whose station in life placed them far above her. He drew a deep breath and leaned back in his chair. "Even my cousin, Aaron, our host, does not know the details of my story, since I am older than he, and our families have been separated by distance and time."

Seven pairs of eyes anchored him in place. He relaxed, closed his eyes, and began.

"My childhood was one of privilege, rich with learning and wisdom. I grew up in the royal residence in Toledo. My father was a famous physician tending to the health of aristocrats. He and the other court physicians provided the most advanced and effective medical care in the world. Their tradition drew from the ancient knowledge of the Mesopotamians, Babylonians, Persians, Hindus, Greeks, and Egyptians.

"Toledo is an ancient city. At its heart is the esteemed School of Translators. All around me, scholarly men studied the arts and sciences. They were mainly Arabs and Jews, but there were also a few Christians. The Castilian Christians believed their beliefs were superior, even though the Arabs and Jews had lived in Toledo long before Christianity ever existed. I was educated with the other children of the palace. As a child I showed no aptitude for medicine, nor did I have any interest in it. Since I was Jewish, Hebrew my first language. We spoke it at home and at synagogue. The dominant culture of Toledo had been Mozarab Muslims for centuries, so Arabic was spoken all around me.

"I was educated together with the children of Jews, Arabs, and Christians. As a youth I absorbed the languages around me as easily as a sponge sops up water. Our teachers held us to the highest academic standards. As a rash youth, I was accustomed to stealing away from my studies, dressed in clothing more suited to a tradesman than an aristocrat, and taking late-night jaunts in the back streets of Toledo with the Castilian and Arab boys of the court. They had more freedom, as there were many restrictions placed on Jews. But we were all privileged youths and determined that such rules did not apply to us. We ignored the regulations with impunity. Yet, apart from my friends, most others held a deep-seated belief that Jews were somehow different. Among my friends however, we were all equal. We were masters at deceiving our teachers and parents. When my father discovered my transgressions, he made sure I knew the history of our people. He educated me with a detailed litany of the persecutions the Jews had endured both long ago and very recently, and why it was dangerous for me to carouse with the other boys. But running with the Christian boys taught me much about the world beyond the palace walls and inspired my curiosity about the lives of ordinary people. He forbade me, for my own safety, to go out at night and encouraged me to be more serious about my studies.

"Though medicine did not appeal to me, I had an aptitude for languages and became adept at Latin, Castilian, Hebrew, Greek, and Arabic and their various alphabets. I loved the serenity of the scriptorium where rows of scholars stood side by side, translating the wisdom of the ages. We converted ancient treatises on astronomy, algebra, geometry, and celestial motions, written by the wisest men of their ages. Most of these works were written in Greek. We translated them into Latin, Hebrew, and Castilian. In this way many more scholars could access the wisdom of the ages. I personally worked on transcribing Ptolemy's Almagest, but others worked on compositions by Archimedes, Euclid, and Al-Razi.

"The Castilian king is a man of wisdom with a great love of learning. He himself has written scholarly works, and a lovely work of poetry dedicated the Christian Holy Mother Mary. He sent orders to Toledo that I should deliver several of these priceless works to his court in Burgos. He trusted no one below my station to deliver them. These parchments are priceless. For this reason, I have come to Burgos. Now you understand why it was so crucial that you returned the parchment to me."

"May I see it?" Mateo asked. "I regret that my education was cut short. Seeing one of these venerable works would be a great privilege."

"Let's unroll it and I'll tell you what it says." Samuel suggested. "Johanna, could you please create a space for us at the table?"

Johanna snapped her fingers to summon the servants, who quickly cleared the table. Samuel rolled out a thin, velvety parchment of the finest calfskin. His guests and his children crowded around the document.

"It's so soft," Amika said, touching the edges of the document. She scrutinized the sinuous characters strewn like snakes across the page. "What language is this?"

"This is Arabic. Like the undulating characters of its writing, the Arabic language flows like a melody. It is subtle, full of double entendre, equally suited to sublime poetry and the exacting precision of science."

"What does it say?" Aaron's young daughter asked.

"These parchments hold the words of Maimonides, the most famous Hebrew scholar. Sadly, he left this world fifty years ago. He was revered as a scientist, philosopher, astronomer, and physician. At an early age he had already read the works of Greek philosophers available in Arabic. Though Jewish, he swam in the deep waters of

Islamic learning and culture. The words your fingers are touching are an excellent example of his wisdom. 'We each decide whether to make ourselves learned or ignorant, compassionate or cruel, generous or miserly. We are responsible for what we are.'" Samuel paused. A sober silence filled the room.

"At the behest of Alfonso the Learned, King of Castile, I have translated Maimonides' works into Latin so that he might share in this wisdom. You see, Amika and Mateo," Samuel continued "recovering this document was of utmost importance. If it had been lost, all the civilized world would have mourned. I want to give you something to express my deepest gratitude."

He reached under his cloak and withdrew a small pouch. "Go ahead, open it," he said, handing to Mateo.

Mateo reached out to accept the velvet sac. With delicate fingers he withdrew five gold coins inscribed in Latin with an image of a grand castle on one side and a lion with swishing tail on the other. "Five maravedi?" Mateo's eyes bounced from the coins in his palm to the face of the scholarly Jewish gentleman before him. "That is most generous of you." Mateo dispensed with the customary three rejections proper decorum required. "We are deeply grateful."

"There is one more coin I want to give you," Samuel said, holding the coin by its edge as a priest holds the Eucharist. "This one is for you, Amika." At its center was an embossed image of a tree with a broad canopy and spreading roots. "This is the tree of life. It is an ancient symbol of the unity of all people and all things under God." He gently placed the coin in Amika's hand.

"You may do with this whatever you like. It is feely given. But it would be my fondest wish that you place it with your other gifts at the base of the Cruz de Ferro. Though I am not a Christian, God's love embraces us all. There are many roads to wisdom, just as there are many paths to heaven. God hears but one voice in the prayers of all people. Tomorrow we part ways. I am glad our paths crossed. I will stay here with my cousin for a while before returning to Toledo. But I wish you safe travels."

The following morning, the two travelers who left Aaron's home looked nothing like the two vagabonds who had entered the previous day. Gone were the tattered nun's habit and the remnants of the once-elegant padded vest. They now wore fine linen tunics and woolen cloaks. Each had a broad-brimmed leather hat to keep the rain and sun off their heads. Bulbous drinking gourds dangled from their stout walking sticks.

"Where did you find these?" Amika asked Johanna.

"We have many friends here who owe us 'favors,' shall we say." Johanna winked at Aaron as if sharing a private joke. "Many doors are closed to us. Samuel enjoys far more freedom to choose his profession in Toledo than we have in Burgos. Yet we provide services to wealthy clients not permitted to Christians. They find our services helpful, particularly when they encounter a gambling debt or need to silence rumors of bad behavior. When the almighty closes a door another is opened."

Johanna placed her hands firmly on Amika's shoulders and held her at arm's length inspecting her pilgrim's costume. With one finger she delicately lifted the simple necklace around Amika's neck.

"What is this?" she wondered out loud.

Instinctively Amika raised her fingertips to her neck. "My mother wove it from her own hair when I was a young child."

"Hmmmm, very interesting. There is much I don't know of the Basque traditions, but this seems a worthy gift, a deeply personal tie binding mother to child. You must cherish it."

"Yes," Amika closed her eyes. "This is the last memento I have of my mother." She tossed her head, shaking the memory away. "You have been so kind, what can I do to even the scales?" Gratitude tempered by a sense of indebtedness roiled Amika's heart.

"Please, don't fret. I am happy to help a fellow traveler on the path. We will not forget you. If you ever need help, we will be here for you." Johanna brusquely dropped her tender demeanor and pointed Amika toward the door. Have safe journeys, B'ezrat HaShem, if God wills it."

"Safe journeys," Samuel echoed

Amika and Mateo headed westward leaving the city of Burgos and climbed the final hill before reaching the endless plateau called the meseta. The magnificent, unfinished walls of the Burgos Cathedral glowed in the slanting lemony rays of morning as they left the Jewish quarter behind and made their way back to the Camino. By afternoon ominous clouds obscured the sun. They quickly recognized the true value of the pilgrim clothing Johanna had given them when rain and wind swirled around them.

CHAPTER TEN

Three sets of eyes peered out from the shelter of a rock ledge as a torrential rain pummeled the slope before them.

"What do we do now?" a small, reedy voice asked.

"We just stay right here, stay dry, and wait out the storm," Amika replied.

Only an hour ago, when the afternoon rainfall became a deluge, Amika and Mateo ran a short distance up the slope to take refuge under a rock ledge protruding from the hillside. They found the space already occupied by a young girl of perhaps seven years hunched in the shallow cave. As thin as a broomstick, the girl wrapped her arms around her knees and shivered. Amika and Mateo huddled on either side of her, sharing their warmth.

Next to the girl lay the lifeless body of a woman curled in a fetal position. Judging from the condition of the corpse, the woman had died very recently. The stench of decay had not yet set in. Her face was covered with open sores. Her fingers were almost black, and several were truncated as if they had been amputated. Raised patches of discolored skin freckled her arms and legs. Amika bent down to look at the dead woman's face but drew back in horror. A bulbous growth of swollen skin bulged from her face where her nose should have been. Amika gently pulled the woman's head scarf over her face to hide it.

"I knew you would come. I have been praying. Mother said she would not leave me alone, and here you are." The little girl's voice was thin and flat. A dirty draw-string tunic hung shapelessly over her thin shoulders. A wild bird's nest of dishwater brown hair framed her somber face, pale as ashes. She tucked her chin close to her chest, accentuating her wide forehead. Eyes like a stormy sea stared unblinking into the murky tempest.

Amika and Mateo looked at each other over the girl's head. "Your mother?" Amika asked, indicating the dead woman with a nod in the direction of the body.

"She was sick. She had a disease. We were walking to Santiago to beg for a miracle, but we did not make it. In the end, I could not recognize her. She had been very pretty. Now . . ." She trailed off. "It started as a red rash but grew into blisters." The girl squirmed between Amika and Mateo seated on either side of her. She buried her face in the cradle her skirt made stretched between her knees and shuddered. Amika laid a kind hand between her protruding shoulder blades.

"Soon she was covered with them," the girl continued. "Her fingers and nose shriveled. She screamed with pain when I tried to touch her."

Leprosy, Amika thought.

"She tried to walk but her bones were too weak. A kind man told us where to find the Lazarus monastery of San Anton. He said the monks there would look after her. She tried but could not hold off death long enough. Last night when it started raining, we crawled up here. My mother told me to be brave and promised me someone would find me and take care of me." The girl lifted her face, looking from Amika to Mateo with perfect innocence. Her guiltless eyes searched their faces.

"What is your name?" Mateo asked.

"Esperanza."

"Your mother was a wise woman," Amika said. "She named you for the virtue of hope. Have you eaten?"

"Only a crust of bread another pilgrim offered us yesterday morning. Mother gave her piece to me."

"In the morning I will find food for us," Amika promised. "Then we will lay your mother to rest. But now we will sleep. You are safe, Esperanza." Amika crooned tenderly. "You're right. Your mother did send us to you." *Just as my mother sent Ane to me,* Amika thought. The idea comforted her. Perhaps she could repay the love Ane had shown her with the kindness she would offer Esperanza.

99

Amika reached a hand out to Mateo. He tenderly enveloped hers in his own. He wrapped his cloak around all three of them, and they slept, sharing their warmth.

In the murky half-light just before dawn Amika strode out on a hillside of dewy grass. The countryside was nothing like the familiar mountains of her Pyrenees home, but she was sure she could find something to stave off hunger. Rolling pastures dotted with golden fields of ripe grain created a pastoral checkerboard. She pivoted full circle, taking in her surroundings. Farther up the hill an uncultivated stand of patchy forest clung to existence. Sunlight streamed through the branches. Bushes and flowers dotted the understory. *Here*, she thought, *I will find breakfast.* When she returned to Mateo and Esperanza, her skirt cradled a profusion of small white mushrooms, hawthorn berries, apple mint, and the nutlike roots of water grass.

Mateo had also risen and left the rock shelter. He removed his cloak, tucked it around the sleeping Esperanza and walked up the hillside searching for a suitable resting place for Esperanza's unlucky mother. A short distance up the hill a lone sycamore stood separated from the woodland above. An ample canopy of broad leaves shaded its smooth, dappled bark. Knotty roots radiated out from the trunk, leaving gullies of soft grass nestled between. Mateo found a fallen branch to use as a crude digging stick and hollowed out a shallow grave between the buried roots.

Amika and Mateo returned to find Esperanza wrapped in Mateo's cloak, sobbing quietly curled up next to her mother's body.

"We are here." Amika bent to brush tears from the girl's face. "Did you think we had abandoned you?"

"No," Esperanza's voice quavered like a warbler's tremulous song. "I was sleeping. In my dream, I heard my mother speak to me from beyond. She asked me to lay with her one last time. Her voice was thin and far away. She reached out to touch my cheek at the same moment when you wiped away my tears. It was as if she used your fingers as her own to reach out and touch me." Esperanza sat up and heaved a heavy sigh.

"I have prepared a quiet spot for her final resting place." Mateo gently wrapped the mother's body in his cloak. The three of them formed a quiet procession up the hill. They laid the mother's ravaged body in its grave at the base of the sycamore and covered her as best they could with late summer wildflowers and loose soil.

"Eternal rest grant onto her and let perpetual light shine upon her," Mateo said.

All was silent. A narrow slash of pale yellow broke over a band of slate gray clouds, the last of yesterday's storm, resting on the horizon as the sun struggled into the sky. They shared the breakfast Amika had gathered for them, then trundled down the hill to rejoin other pilgrims on the path westward.

Like a silken ribbon, the path draped itself over the rolling plateau, rising and falling, appearing on the hilltops, and disappearing again into the dales. Tiny villages of a dozen or so somber stone houses hunkered alongside pens of muddy ewes with half-grown lambs roughly butting their udders. Each fortified hilltop town bristled with church steeples and battlements. They traversed swampy lowlands where insects buzzed in the waning warmth of summer, eager to lay their eggs before cold weather set in. About midday they reached the outskirts of a town where a dozen townsmen stoked fiery-hot pottery kilns crowded with colorfully glazed tiles and utilitarian earthenware. Amika, Mateo, and Esperanza stopped for a few moments to watch as the men stoked fires in their round kilns and gently moved the pottery to the center of the ovens where the heat was perfect. They walked on. At the far edge of town was a monastery with a small hospice, San Lazaro.

"That's it," Esperanza declared.

"That's what?" Amika responded.

"That's the hospice my mother and I tried to reach. Other pilgrims told us that if she could get to this place the monks would take her in." Esperanza trailed her fingers along the stone façade

101

separating the afflicted from the rest of society until she reached a leper's peep. A grate covered an opening cut away from a corner of the building allowing all who passed to peer inside. Esperanza grasped the iron bars and stoically watched the lepers going about their lives, lowering a bucket into the well, sitting on a bench against a sunny wall, gossiping in little clusters, their misshapen hands pawing the air, seemingly unperturbed by the disfigurements of their fellow sufferers. A ringing bell called them to Sext, the noon prayer service, and they all disappeared into the chapel.

A few moments passed as Amika and Mateo stood respectfully apart from the girl, allowing her to grieve. Then, Mateo touched her shoulder.

"Your mother's resting place is peaceful and beautiful." Mateo's hand on her back was assurance itself. "Being separated from you in this leper's *refugio* would not have made her final days better. At least she had you by her side in her last hours."

Esperanza turned from the monastery, wordlessly took Amika's hand, and shuffled away. They walked for hours through luxuriant golden fields ready for reaping. The wind-rippled crops briefly bowed their heads at its touch.

That night they found a simple pilgrim's meal and a bunk in the *dormitorio* of the San Esteban monastery. The atmosphere at dinner was charged with apprehension as nine pilgrims shared gossip about the path ahead. Four Benedictine monks clustered at one end of the long trestle table, immersed in conversation.

A burly brother with a dark beard spreading across his face, who looked like he would be more comfortable at a blacksmith's forge than fingering rosary beads, spoke. "I have heard rumors that there are robbers along the trail."

A tall, ginger-haired brother was also worried. "It's no wonder there are robbers here. There are very few villages along this stretch of the road. The sad settlements we have passed lately are tiny and poor. The lonely stretches between grow longer."

A scrawny, beardless monk barely lifted his eyes from his plate, too nervous to eat, until an elderly, white-haired monk gently patted his arm. "Brother Raul, don't you have faith that God will protect us?" Unlike some aged folks whose worldly wisdom made them irascible, Brother Alfonso seemed to be perpetually mildly amused.

Across the table, a gaunt woman clutching the hand of her crippled son, listened with obvious anxiety. She directed her comments to the kindly, white-haired monk. "May I walk with you? My son and I are alone. We would be easy prey for robbers."

"Of course, my child," Brother Alfonso answered.

Mateo broke into their conversation. "I have seen no Templars for many days. Though they are almost as much a threat as the bandits themselves, their presence discourages all but the most brazen brigands. It is best if we walk together. It's harder to attack a group."

Heads nodded up and down the table as the pilgrims and the brothers eyed one another, taking the measure of those who would now become their companions.

Next morning Amika, Mateo, and Esperanza set out in the company of six other pilgrims. For many miles no one spoke, preferring to cluster with known companions. The four Benedictine Brothers walked in a tight bunch, keeping to themselves but within sight of the others. Amika and Mateo each held one of Esperanza's hands. Their crunching footfalls drummed a steady cadence, as comforting as a rocking cradle. At midday they pulled off the track to rest in a field of ripe barley. Each pilgrim rummaged in pockets and pouches for a piece of the dense brown bread hoarded from last night's meal.

"We all stole a piece of bread," Esperanza giggled. "We are a band of thieves." The others smiled sheepishly, casting guilty sidelong glances at each other.

As they rested, a handsome, fresh-faced young man sauntered along the trail toward them. Every face watched him approach. He stopped in front of them, eyeing each one in turn.

103

"Mind if I join you?" Not waiting for an answer, he opened his bulging pack and withdrew a lute with a belly as round as a sow's belly and a headstock shaped like a sickle.

"The weather is fair." He smiled broadly. "Much better than yesterday. The path was so slick with rain I almost dropped my instrument in a deep puddle. Luckily, another pilgrim checked my fall. That sounds like reason enough to celebrate with a song, doesn't it?" His ruddy face, ringed by wispy brown curls, glowed as he gave Esperanza a mischievous wink. Esperanza tittered and blushed.

> *"Well, everyone needs a sunny day*
> *And everyone needs to get away*
> *Sunshine falls on those at play*
> *And pilgrims walking along the Way*
> *So let us tell a joke or two*
> *And I will play a son for you."*

The performance earned him a round of happy applause, and smiles blossomed on every face.

"Normally, I'd pass the hat and ask you to express your gratitude with coin," he said with a grin. "But the little girl has loosened my heartstrings a little." He gave Esperanza a broad, toothy smile. "Allow me to introduce myself. I am Tulio, singer of songs, player of games, entertainer of nobles and peasants alike." He snatched a slouchy beret from his head and bowed. He beamed at the strange assortment of pilgrims, four Benedictine monks, a mother towing her disabled son in a wooden wheelbarrow and a threesome he assumed were a family—mother, father, and doe-eyed daughter.

Ernesto, the brawny bearded brother, spoke up. "We cannot sing you a rousing tune. We are only monks, but at least we can give you our blessing. Gather around."

The pilgrims circled around him. Esperanza moved to the front of the group, knelt piously before him, and bowed her head. Amika and Mateo lingered on the periphery. Ernesto nodded to the elder brother. Brother Alfonso extended his long arms over their heads as if to shelter them. *"In nomine Patris et Filii et Spiritus Sancti,"* he intoned, gently touching his head, heart, and shoulders in the sign of the cross. "Dear Lord, we beg you to bless us. This band of pilgrims seeks to honor you with every step along this sacred path. We pray for your guidance and protection."

The pilgrims responded with a hearty "Amen." Armed with God's blessing and Tulio's good cheer, they walked on lightheartedly.

They resumed their walk, succumbing once again to the cadence of footsteps on pebbles, each lost in his separate world. Esperanza sidled up to the boy in the wheelbarrow. She scrutinized him with unselfconscious curiosity. He was a few years older than she; his torso and arms were lanky and awkward, as were most boys his age. But his thin legs laid in a useless tangle in the bed of the cart.

"What's your name?" Esperanza asked.

"I'm Ignacio."

"What happened to your legs?" she asked with the ingenuous innocence of a child.

The boy tilted his narrow face with its hawksbill nose up toward her. A thick shock of auburn curls hung down to his thin shoulders. His abundant hair seemed to be the only riches he possessed. Though clean, his shapeless tunic was of the crudest hemp fabric. The wheelbarrow in which he slouched consisted of a basic plank platform mounted on one large, wooden wheel. An undyed woolen blanket protected him from splinters.

"We don't know," he replied. "It came on suddenly. I was a normal boy, tending sheep, feeding chickens, and fishing in the stream with my friends after Sunday Mass. A few months ago, I started dropping things. My hands and legs began to tingle. Soon I became so weak I could barely grip my spoon. Within weeks my legs had grown so feeble I could no longer stand. The village priest suggested our only hope was to throw ourselves upon the Lord's mercy by making this pilgrimage to Santiago. My mother suffers so," he confided. "She is not strong but has pushed me for several weeks. Many kind pilgrims have helped us along the way. Whether we make it to Santiago or not, whether I am cured or not, we have learned that there is much goodness in the world."

The boy's mother stopped, set down the handles of the barrow, and turned to face Esperanza. The four monks, Amika, and Mateo stopped also. She eyed the little girl with fascination. "Who are you, child?"

Esperanza paused, staring up at the woman. Her wide-set eyes riveted the woman in place. Her voice became as grave and low as a grown woman's. "You are expecting a miracle," she answered. "You shall have your miracle, though it may not be the one you seek."

The troupe stared in wonder at the girl's transformation and her prophesy.

"We know Saint James has appeared to many along the Way and performed miracles." The woman pressed on, ignoring Esperanza's ominous prediction. "Have you heard these stories?"

"Your name is Soledad, meaning solitude," Esperanza continued. "But by the grace of God your solitude will end soon." Esperanza heaved great sigh. She took a deep breath and shed her solemn demeanor as a wet dog shakes off water.

The four Benedictine brothers gaped at the little girl. Raul, the youngest of them, spoke up, reinforcing Esperanza's message. "Yes, I believe you will get your miracle. The Lord works in mysterious ways. And sometimes he sends unlikely messengers." He spoke with a light tone, as if little girls making prophesies was an everyday occurrence. "We all hope that she is right, don't we?" The four Brothers nodded. "Well then, we can choose to believe in this miracle, can't we?" He searched the others' faces. "Good. We will pray for you, Soledad and Ignacio."

"I heard of one miracle quite like the one you seek." Everyone turned to look at the tall brother whose bristly ginger hair and beard stuck out from his head as stiff as porcupine quills. "It happened many years ago. There was a man who, for thirteen years, endured the same hardship as your son. He was a wealthy man, so he rode a horse in comfort to Santiago. The priests at the Cathedral of Santiago told him to keep vigil in the church. For thirteen days he kept his vigil, one day for each year of his paralysis. He never left the cathedral. Upon hearing of his mission, other pilgrims brought him food and tended to his needs. On the thirteenth day Saint James appeared. He spoke to the man kindly for a while, then knelt before him. He stretched out one of the man's constricted legs, then the other. The cathedral was crowded that day with pilgrims from many lands. Each of them heard the saint's words in his own language, though the saint spoke only to the crippled man. For the first time in thirteen years the man stood. Out of gratitude he walked all the way home, never riding the horse."[i]

"Thank you, Brother," breathed the boy's mother. "You have renewed my faith. For all their apparent piety, most pilgrims do not believe in miracles. But I know miracles do happen."

"Yes, they do. I will pray you see your own miracle come true." Brother Juan gave a slight bow toward Soledad. The other monks followed; their palms pressed together as if in prayer. Now it seemed that the four brothers shared a mission—to stay with Soledad and Ignacio in hopes of witnessing the anticipated miraculous cure.

Without a word Mateo picked up the handles of the wheelbarrow and started walking. Amika walked at Soledad's side in silence. For several days, the band of pilgrims continued walking from dawn until dusk, pausing only at midday to eat their pilfered bread, make a tea from the leaves Amika gathered, and give thanks.

Esperanza kept the boy company. Soon the children were telling riddles and devising little games and contests. Who would see the first bird in the morning? Who could count the highest? Who could hold their gaze the longest without blinking? The sound of children's laughter tumbled across the rolling plains of the meseta.

Esperanza was everyone's favorite. The youngest brother, Raul, a tall beardless monk was a wizard with a pocketknife and whittled a pair of swords from soft willow branches for the children,

107

complete with hilts bearing heraldic crests. Mock battles ensued as they smacked their toy swords against each other.

On the third day it rained. The mood became more serious as the path became slick with mud. On a path of smooth stones laid down by Roman soldiers who occupied the country hundreds of years before, they forded a rivulet running across the road. They hopped from one rain-slick paver to the next. The last person to cross was Soledad. Stepping off the last stone, her foot slipped out from under her. She landed flat on her back; her head bounced on the wet rock. She did not rise. Though her eyes were open, and she appeared to be conscious, she did not move. The brothers immediately clustered around her.

"Be careful. Do not pick her up. She might have broken bones." One of the brothers stepped in. "I am Brother Ernesto. In our community I oversee the infirmary." He spoke with the voice of authority. Everyone obeyed him instantly.

He knelt beside her in the mud. "Dear lady, Can you hear me?"

"Yes," she replied.

"Can you see my hand?" He extended his long index finger and moved it slowly from right to left across her field of vision. The woman's eyes tracked back and forth following the finger's movement.

Again "yes" was the answer.

Gingerly, the monk moved first one of her arms then the other. He bent her right knee, then her left. "Does this cause you pain?"

"No. I think I'm fine."

He motioned for Brother Juan to help him. Together they eased her into a sitting position, then lifted her to her feet. She wobbled and swayed. But after a few moments began walking slowly and carefully. Mateo gave her his walking stick and the group walked into the gathering darkness.

Feathery, wind-shredded mare's-tail clouds streaked the sky as the light faded and the wind rose. Delayed by Soledad's fall, it was clear the group would not reach the safe harbor of an inn or monastery that night. All eyes scanned the horizon, searching for shelter. Brother Raul was the first to spot a refuge.

"Look there!" he called out above the wind. "I think it's a shepherd's hut."

Silhouetted against the darkening horizon a small enclosure burrowed into the hillside. Irregular rock slabs teetered on each other's shoulders without the benefit of mortar; its low-slung doorway was so small one needed to hunch over to enter. Inside was a tiny fire pit, with a crude chimney, barely tall enough to peep above the overlying grass.

"It's not much, but it's better than sleeping in the barley fields," Tulio declared.

"At least it's warm and dry," Amika replied.

"You can entertain us with a song," Esperanza chirped hopefully.

Within the hour, the group of ten weary pilgrims huddled inside the tiny building. The smell of sheep dung mingled with the odor of charred mutton and the crush of human bodies. A few cobs of corn littering the ground inside the tiny refuge spared the travelers from hunger. Tulio strummed a gentle lullaby as the motley troupe sheltered from the restless sky.

"Do you hear that?" Ignacio whispered urgently to Soledad.

"It's nothing," she replied, eager to close her eyes and drift off.

"No, it's something. Shhh." He hushed them all as he strained to hear the distant sound.

"Wolves!" Soledad replied. "Don't worry, we will be safe in here."

"No," Esperanza murmured. "It's not wolves."

All ears followed the distant sounds. To their left they heard yipping; then a low growl rumbled to their right. Behind them, much closer now, a doglike bark rang out.

"No, these are not wolves. These are robbers." Esperanza was uncannily certain.

A shock of recognition rippled from one person to the next. Wolf yips and barks came closer, followed by the muffled scuffling of feet.

"They're stuffing the chimney with dried stems," Amika hissed. Clots of dried mud and chunks of stone rained down the chimney into the fire pit.

A few moments later they smelled it, the scent of burning grass. Almost immediately, smoke engulfed the cramped shelter.

"Hurry," Mateo ordered, "or we will soon have no air to breathe." Grabbing his walking stick he bolted out the door and scrambled to the roof of the hut, searching the darkness for their attackers. "Get out! Now!" He called to the others as he drove the butt of his staff through the chimney dislodging the burning dross.

They emerged coughing and sputtering.

"We must smother the flames, if we don't want a prairie fire to flare up." Mateo warned.

Amika dug her hands into the earth and shoveled small heaps of dirt onto the embers and smoldering cinders. Soledad joined her. Furiously they scooped and tossed, scooped and tossed damp earth through the low doorway. Deprived of air, the fire choked then died. Out in the open, they were now as exposed as naked children to the predatory robbers.

Esperanza stood in front of the smoking hut. The dying fire backlit her small body and smoke billowed around her as if she stood before the gates of hell. The other pilgrims clustered around the small child, dazed, and confused.

"God forgives you," she called into the night. "You are poor and hopeless men. In your desperation you have turned to evil ways. We are poor pilgrims. You thought you could smoke us out, and rob us, and here we are, unharmed. God is with us. He has protected us. We have nothing to offer you but our prayers." Shuffling feet closed in. Shadowy figures emerged from the darkness. Gaunt faces sat atop bony shoulders. The smoke-filled air painted them a ghostly gray.

"I have saved this crust of bread for tomorrow's breakfast." Esperanza held the heel of a rounded loaf on her outstretched palm. "Who needs this the most?"

Wordlessly, a scarecrow of a man pushed his scrawny son forward. The boy's stomach bulged. His round eyes dominated his hollow-cheeked face. Esperanza placed the crust of bread in his hand. Food emerged from pockets and folds of the other pilgrims' clothing.

"We will pray for you now," Brother Alfonso murmured.

The four monks, rosaries in hand, began chanting. "Our Father who art in heaven, hallowed be they name ... Forgive us our trespasses as we forgive those who trespass against us," they droned on.

"Go in peace," Esperanza's clear voice rang out like bells at midnight.

The would-be robbers melted back into the night. The sounds of shuffling feet faded into the profound silence of an onyx sky. Though stillness returned, tranquility did not. The pilgrims realized that they would face a long, famished day ahead.

"I will scour the river edges and mossy slopes tomorrow," Amika reassured them. "We may be hungry, but we will not starve."

Esperanza edged up next to Ignacio, who sat in the dirt, leaning his back against the wall of the hut.

"You are as brave as a mastiff defending his flocks," the boy marveled. "How did you come to be so fearless?"

Esperanza shrugged her thin shoulders. "I'm not brave. I simply do what my voices direct me to do."

"Your voices?" Ignacio recoiled.

"Well, not voices. It is my mother's voice. She tells me not to fear because I will be taken care of. I am not brave. I have faith."

"My mother has faith." Ignacio sighed. "She believes what the priest told her. For my part, I'm not so sure. The paralysis came on so suddenly. At first, I thought I was being punished. Though I am not a

111

perfect son, I have committed no mortal sin. All the usual explanations—God works in mysterious ways; there is a reason for everything; the sins of the fathers are visited on the sons—I do not believe any of them. My father was a violent drunk who finally drank himself to death. Why should I be punished instead of him? There is no reason for it!" He growled angrily. Color rose in Ignacio's cheeks and his breathing quickened.

Esperanza looked deep into his soft, mahogany eyes and reached up to touch his auburn curls. "I'm sorry." Then she leaned back against the wall.

When the black of night bled into the dark indigo of earliest dawn, Amika rose from the nest she had made for herself with her cloak. She trudged off to the boggy edges of the slow-moving river that hugged the trail in search of something to replace the bread they had given the starving robbers. By the time the others were waking she was ready to dole out little nutlike bulbs she had dug up. She watched as her companions' faces registered surprise, bewilderment, even disgust, but they chewed, nonetheless. They chewed and chewed.

"There is no way to eat these quickly she explained. "Eat them slowly to savor their unique taste."

Mateo raised his eyebrows and pursed his lips as his jaw worked them over. "They taste rather creamy."

"I'd say nutty." Brother Alfonso nodded in agreement.

"They are certainly chewy, crisp on the outside and soft in the middle," Soledad said. "What are they?"

"They are little bulbs growing on the roots of a plant called chufa." Amika answered. "The only other time I have eaten them was when I was starving." Puzzled faces turned toward her, but she offered no further explanation.

Brother Ernesto was more skeptical. "Thank you, Amika. We are grateful." He looked dubiously at the small tubers in his palm. "Please do not take offence, but I for one am looking forward to a hearty stew with our fellow Benedictine Brothers at the monastery in

Sahagun. We should be there by evening. We will be well fed and safe." He surreptitiously dropped his chufa into the bushes.

A brisk, warm wind scoured the last traces of last night's smoky aroma from the air and replaced it with the clean, dry scent of wheat fields ready for reaping.

Brother Ernesto approached Mateo, who was pushing Ignacio's wheelbarrow. Soledad, never far from her son, walked beside them. Ernesto's black robes shifted in the breeze, making his rosary's crucifix dance around his waist. "Please forgive us for not properly introducing ourselves and for staying so much to ourselves. We are monks and as part of our vows we refrain from idle chatter as much as possible. I am Brother Ernesto." He extended his hand to Mateo, man to man. Mateo hesitated, looking at the brother's smooth skin, unblemished by hard labor. He rested the wheelbarrow on the ground and clasped Brother Ernesto's proffered handshake with his own scarred hand.

"My name is Mateo, stone carver of Jaen."

"Let me push the wheelbarrow today. I am strong." Brother Ernesto smiled, patting his generous belly, as if his girth gave his strength.

Mateo nodded. "Thank you. I am grateful for your help."

The pilgrims gathered their belongings and their courage and resumed their walk.

As the sun approached its zenith, Ignacio called to the others. "Where is Amika? She's been gone since breakfast."

"She's foraging for our lunch," Esperanza answered. "She will meet us on the road in a little while." Mateo bent his knees, took her small chin between thumb and forefinger, and lifted her face to his.

"How do you know this?" he asked. "This time I want a real answer, not some mumbo jumbo about hearing voices."

113

Esperanza looked disappointed. "I thought you understood," she whimpered. "I told you. My mother speaks to me. Do you think I'm lying?"

Mateo dropped his hand and stroked her unkempt hair. "I'm sorry. I do not think you are lying. I am a man of many disappointments and little faith."

"It will be well." The girl patted his hand in consolation. "You don't need to understand everything for it to be true. Amika will catch up with us soon."

When the sun was high, Amika appeared over the horizon. As she approached the group her broad smile lit up the world around her. She held the edges her skirt up to form a basket, exposing her dirty knees. Her tunic bowed under the weight of late summer edibles.

"Well, you've found us." Mateo stepped forward, arms extended, as if to embrace her, caught himself short, then abruptly dropped his arms. "What have you here?" He searched the contents of her skirt then quickly averted his eyes from her bare legs.

Amika grinned. "I've been on a hunting expedition." "Look what I've found—oyster thistle, fennel tubers, blackthorn berries—late summer gifts from a copse of bushes in a moist wash."

Her heart caught on her ribs when she noticed Mateo's eyes wandering over her bare legs. She swiveled around so her back faced him, and called out, "Would anyone like something for lunch?"

The unexpected bounty banished the foul humors left by the previous night's raid. By mid-afternoon they had reached the ruins of an old Roman bath. Mateo became tour guide as they meandered through once-elegant rooms, each paved with stunning images and patterns.

"These are called mosaics."

"I've never seen anything like it," Amika marveled. "Look how the tiny pieces fit so tightly together."

"Unless you've been to the Roman provinces of Italia, you could not have seen anything like these."

"I know we have been walking on sections of the old Roman

Road, but I never imagined I would see remains of buildings they left behind," Ignacio spoke up.

"In the southern provinces of Iberia, where I grew up, the Romans left many structures like these."

"What happened to them? Where did they go?" Amika asked.

"Long ago, they drifted away from greatness. Groups fought each other for power and wealth. They became so weak they were unable to defend themselves when invaders from the north swooped down on them. Their civilization died, but they left us these beautiful remnants."

Amika tip-toed across floors inlaid with intricate, multi-colored patterns—faces of wild-haired deities riding on tempestuous winds, fishes and eels writhing in turbulent seas, men who looked like kings, and elegant women.

The wanderers tucked themselves into a corner of the remaining walls to enjoy a quiet meal. Their tranquility was shattered when a boisterous pack of five young men poured over the walls, shouting to each other.

"Look at this one, it looks like a checkerboard."

"And this one is braided like rope."

They swarmed through the roofless rooms enthusiastically until they discovered the pilgrims huddling in their corner.

"What have we here? Who are you?" All five gaped at the ragged pilgrims.

"We are pilgrims on our way to Santiago," Mateo explained simply. "The question is who are you?"

The boys grinned at each other. "We are brothers."

Amika scrutinized the boys. They all looked close to the same age. Normally there would be at least ten years between oldest and youngest of five children, and then only if there were no dead babies between them.

115

"No, you're not brothers," she openly defied their story. "You're too close together in age to be brothers."

They did not take offense at her skepticism but laughed and slapped each other's backs.

"Yes, we're all brothers with the same father, but with four different mothers."

"You expect us to believe that?" Soledad scolded.

"Yes, it is easy to explain, though not a simple situation. Our father was an itinerant tinsmith. He traveled all over our native country of Galicia. We saw him only when he visited. He never stayed in one place more than a few weeks. When he died our mothers traveled to his funeral in his hometown where our mothers discovered they were not his only wife. They were furious. We were only half-grown boys, and of course we were devastated to learn our cheerful, loving father was a despicable philanderer. After the time of mourning had passed, we decided we should meet every year to celebrate his death. We have done so for three years now. Each time we meet, we walk a section of the Camino to do penance for our father's many sins. We decided some good should come of his fornication. We have grown to love each other like the brothers we truly are."

Amika and her group scrutinized the young men. They were as different as chalk and cheese, one with curly black locks and smoldering black eyes. Another was tall and willowy with angular features and wispy brown hair, barely thick enough to cover his pate. The youngest was beardless and freckled with an open, honest face. The remaining two looked like brothers. One's hair was so orange it looked like a carrot newly dug from the ground; the other's was the color of a clay pot. Yet they all had a hint of resemblance. She stared at them, trying to pin down exactly what made them look like brothers despite their obvious differences. Then she hit on it. All of them had a cleft chin. The two carrot-tops had barely a subtle dent, but all of them shared this singular trait.

Amika giggled. Their story was comical unless you were one of the unfortunate mothers. The unusual way they had chosen to deal with their peculiar circumstances was ingenious. Most amusing of all was the dimpled chin that marked them as brothers as surely as if their father's name had been tattooed on their arms at birth.

"So, this year you are walking the meseta?" Soledad inquired.

"Yes, this lonely stretch has challenged our resolve to keep walking," said the curly moreno. "But sharing memories of our departed father keeps us amused and the miles slip under our feet as easily as a toboggan slides over a snowy slope."

"That, and singing our songs," the youngest piped up. "We all know the same bawdy songs—another inheritance from our father. Perhaps not as pious as the Camino warrants, but it passes the time and reinforces our brotherhood."

Ignacio grinned broadly, dragging his body upward to sit straighter in his barrow.

"Hello, young man." The tall willowy brother bent slightly to shake Ignacio's hand. The gesture startled him. Most strangers found him repellant or ignored him entirely. "Do you know any good songs?" the tall brother asked.

Ignacio smiled even wider and bobbed his head. He slid a quick sidelong glance at his mother who merely rolled her eyes and averted her gaze, giving tacit permission for him to unearth one of his father's drunken tunes.

"Oh yes, if the song was sung in the local pub, my father knew it. I know many off-color songs."

"And as a minstrel, I have heard every humorous or debauched song you can think of," Tulio interjected.

"All right then, off we go!" The wispy-haired brother lifted the arms of the wheelbarrow and rolled off across the monotonous landscape with Ignacio in tow.

Soledad's arm shot into the air. "Wait! Ignacio needs me." She jogged to keep up with them. Mateo gently placed a hand on her forearm to stop her.

"This will be good for the boy," he said. "He needs some male companionship, or how will he know how to be a man?"

Soledad was not sure singing dirty drinking songs was the best rite of passage into the world of men. Her head drooped between her hunched shoulders and a sob shuddered through her.

"Don't worry. He is still your boy. But even disabled boys need to grow up."

Soledad, Esperanza, Amika, and Mateo followed at a distance. In the gap between themselves and the young men, the sounds of simple tunes punctuated by hearty guffaws rolled toward them.

Esperanza took Soledad's hand and started walking. Soledad's heart melted when she remembered this was the hand of a motherless child, bravely walking into an unknowable future.

By the time they sat down that evening to share a hearty stew with the Benedictine brothers their spirits were completely restored.

Gray light crept catlike from the eastern horizon across the fields. Amika rose early and tapped lightly on Mateo's cell's door. When she returned to her cell to wake Esperanza, the girl was already up and ready to walk. Before the table was set to serve the other pilgrims, Mateo begged a few pieces of hard cheese and bread still warm from the ovens from the refectory's corpulent baker. The three wayfarers did not wait to eat in the refectory with the others but stepped into the fragrant morning, ready to walk the Camino toward Leon.

Outside the monastery Amika paused, tilted her head back, closed her eyes, and filled her lungs with the scent of ripe grains. Kestrels perched on branches, hunched over like old men, scanning the ground for grasshoppers, and black hawks circled the morning sky, seeking thermals to bear them aloft. The faint music of bells tumbled down the hillside toward them. Gradually, wave upon wave of bleating grew into a tidal wave of sound. A hoard of black-faced merino sheep descended the trail from their high summer pastures headed toward their lower winter fields. Amika, Mateo, and Esperanza watched a flock of hundreds cross the trail.

"We'll need to step carefully. There is more than just mud to look out for." Mateo lifted each foot daintily.

The trio perched on a boulder and ate their bread. As the earth warmed, they returned to the path, walking at a leisurely pace. By midmorning, the musician, Tulio, caught up with them.

"Sing us an ode to the morning," begged Esperanza. "Or maybe a song about sheep. Did you see the huge flock that crossed the trail earlier?"

"I missed seeing the sheep, but I can certainly see the gifts they left behind." He smiled at the haunting little girl. "You want a song? Hmmm. Let me see. Oh yes, I feel a song coming; it's coming. Here it is!" Tulio smiled and drew a flower from his voluminous sleeve. "What's that you say, little flower?" he asked, holding the daisy to his ear. "She says she'll give me a song but it's not for me. I must give it to you." He bowed as he handed the flower to Esperanza.

Then, pulling his lute from its bag, he began extemporizing lyrics to the tune of "Frère Jacques."

> *"Morning sun shines, morning sun shines*
> *Just for you. Just for you.*
> *Bringing gifts of rainbows, paths among the hedgerows*
> *Filled with poo, filled with poo."*

Esperanza laughed heartily, delighted with the scatological humor. Amika and Mateo guffawed like ten-year-olds. Soledad, pushing Ignacio in his wheelbarrow, pulled up alongside them.

"What's so funny?"

Esperanza delightedly repeated the song—twice—until Ignacio snorted with laughter.

They pushed on. Hawks wheeled overhead. A bustard pecked at the seed-head of ripe wheat. Though it was late summer the male bird still strutted, splayed his tail feathers, and stretched his neck, showing off its rusty orange collar. It flapped clumsily off as the walkers approached.

Their attention drifted away from the sky and returned to the mundane. "Did anyone steal enough bread for our lunch?" Esperanza asked.

"I didn't need to steal it," Mateo said. "I visited the baker early this morning and he generously gave me a small loaf for each of us. We won't go hungry today."

Fields of grain waved in the gentle breeze. Sunflowers heads drooped under the weight of their summer bounty. The pilgrims walked on toward Leon.

* * *

The landscape began to change. A broad river nurturing orchards and vineyards flanked the trail. By day's end the walls of a large city loomed into view. At the gates of Leon, Amika, Mateo, and Esperanza caught up with the troop of singing brothers. Soledad quick-stepped to Ignacio's side, enveloping him in her embrace.

"Mother, please." Ignacio gently pushed her away.

Their eyes locked and a ripple of understanding surged through her. Crippled or not, her boy was growing up. *How will he make a life for himself as a man? Who would marry him? Please, Santiago, give my son a miracle."*

Soon they spotted church towers and red tile roofs peeking from within the ancient city walls built by the Romans to protect its Galician gold mines. Leon's city streets did not meander like those of Burgos, but followed straight north-south, east-west grid lines with military precision. Soledad was the first to catch sight of the half-brothers with Ignacio. She hurried to his side. This time she did not try to embrace her son in front of his new friends. They lingered at the western gate, waiting for the four Benedictine brothers.

"I need a little rest," Brother Alfonso said. "I know this city. It will be bustling with activity. There are shopkeepers and traders of all sorts, as well as artisans, money changers, manufacturers. After the tranquility of the meseta, it may be overwhelming."

Amika agreed. "I am still unused to large cities. They turn my head in so many directions it is confusing. I can find my way in all kinds of open country, but cities jangle my nerves, and I lose my bearings."

"I know about this city too." Mateo's eyes became misty at this unexpected reminder of his privileged past. "My instructors told me that there is a huge scriptorium here where monks have copied and decorated many important books. The embellishments are said to be exquisite."

"That's true," Brother Alfonso responded. "Our Benedictine brothers maintain a famous scriptorium here in Leon in the Basilica of San Isidoro. The Holy Spirit truly inspires the beautiful illustrations of the dedicated scribes." Brother Alfonso squared his shoulders and stood a bit taller with pride. "We also maintain a large pilgrim's hospice with seventy beds. The basilica has a noble history. Do you want to hear it?" Alfonso addressed Ignacio as if he was a student. Ignacio lit up like a fire, burning to consume any knowledge that came his way.

"The basilica was built atop an old Roman temple to erase all trace of its pagan origins. Saint Isidoro's remains lie beneath the floor. Over eight hundred years ago, Isidoro was archbishop of Seville. He was the most celebrated academic and theologian of Spain, one of the most learned men of his time. He translated ancient tracts that would otherwise have been lost."

"Like the one Samuel the Jew showed us?" Ignacio asked.

"Yes, like that one." The group had gathered around Brother Alfonso. "When we take vows to become Benedictine monks, we renounce worldly pursuits and dedicate our lives to charity and scholarship in honor of San Isidoro's work. Once we enter the cloister, we live only within its walls, never emerging until death takes us. For the cloistered brothers, this is their life's work."

"Why are you not inside your monastery?" Ignacio was hungry for information.

"We four were ordered to refresh the scriptorium of Monastery of San Xulián of Samos in Galicia. The Brothers there are all aging and cannot continue with their scholarly duties. We are walking in the footsteps of saints to begin our new assignment."

Brother Alfonso scanned the rapt faces of the pilgrims with satisfaction. "Follow me. I will take you to the monastery of San Isidoro, where you will enjoy a hearty stew and a warm bed."

The next morning, the slanting rays of a golden, late-summer dawn found Tulio on the steps of the great Basilica of San Isidoro, serenading the nightjars swooping overhead. His fingers danced like butterflies on blossoms over the strings, plucking an enchanting melody. Behind closed eyelids he vividly imagined lords and ladies dancing in a great hall draped with tapestries and lit by ornate chandeliers weaving in and out of entwining circles, never touching, always flirting, casting subversive smiles and evasive glances at their next romantic conquest. In his vision, at the end of the night a graceful patrician finds a dewy-eyed, virginal young lady and they dance until dawn. The crowd applauds his performance and the lord of the estate fills his pockets with gold.

He lost track of how long he had played, but when he opened his eyes the courtly embodiment of his reverie stood before him. The gold embroidery that rimmed his calf-length jacket glinted in the morning light. A silver scabbard etched with fine filigree tracery swung from his waist. He was of middle age but as tall and stately as the Andalusian stallion upon which he sat. "Who are you, troubadour?"

Tulio rested his lute gently across his knees and peered at the man. "As you can see, I am a musician. My name is Tulio. Have I done something wrong? I will move along if you think I am loitering."

"Do you see the castle on that hilltop?" He ignored Tulio's question and pointed to a walled town perched on a hill overlooking León. It looked like all the others topping nearly every hill for miles around. "I am the Hidalgo of that place. My palace lies behind those fortifications."

"Hidalgo?" Tulio answered

"Yes, the men of my family have held that title for many generations, a reward for our service to Ferdinand, former king of Leon. Your mastery of your instrument is impressive. My household could use some fresh entertainment. I would like you to come with me and play for my family and our guests."

"Are you serious?" Tulio eyed the patrician suspiciously.

"Are you questioning my honesty?" He leaned back in his saddle and reached for his sheathed sword.

"No, no. Of course not. I did not mean to offend you. I am only surprised by the suddenness of your offer. It's just that I hoped to make it to Santiago before the winter."

"If that is what you are worried about, you need not bother. I was mesmerized by the sensitivity and delicacy of your playing. You should remain the winter with us. We expect Alfonso, the new king and his cohorts to grace us with his presence as colder weather thwarts his military campaigns here in the north. He would appreciate a fine musician."

Alfonso. He is well known as a patron of learning and culture. If he favors me, I might never need to wander the byways again, Tulio thought.

"When should I present myself at your palace?"

"My page will show you the way." He turned to a boy of no more than thirteen. "Raffi," he ordered. "Show this minstrel to the servant's entrance." With that he reined his horse back onto the road out of Leon and disappeared in a dusty blur.

"Come with me," the boy said.

"I would first like to say goodbye to my companions. You may come with me if you like."

123

They made their way back to the monastery where the others were eating a spartan breakfast in silence. The magnitude of the offer settled upon Tulio's mind, and he puffed up with pride as he explained the morning's miracle to the pilgrims. He took his leave amid back-slapping good cheer from all except the girl, Esperanza.

"I wish you would stay with us." She looked downcast. "Who else will pull daisies from their sleeves for me?"

Tulio knelt on one knee to look into her eyes. "Here." He pulled a simple reed whistle from his pouch. "With practice, you will be able to invent your own tunes." He patted her hair. "When you play you will think of me. You ought to be happy for my good fortune. Now I must go."

With that he turned and followed the youth out the eastern gate to the hilltop castle.

CHAPTER ELEVEN

Four days and nights rolled away without incident as water under a bridge. Low stone thatched cottages squatted close to the path. Without Tulio, they were quieter. There was less laughter. The gently rolling landscape of the meseta gave way to long ridges too rugged for crops. Scrub oak, heather, broom, and wild thyme grew in dense tangles along the path, and white quartz striped the rocky soil. On the following night they found refuge at the hospice of San Gregorio, where the Templars garrisoned their knights to protect pilgrims crossing the remote mountain passes.

At the hour when lamps were lit, the bells of the church sounded Vespers. The brothers, hands tucked into their sleeves, cowls raised over their bowed heads, filed into the venerable church. Kneeling on the straw-strewn floor under the barrel-vaulted ceiling of the primitive church they gave thanks for their safe passage. Gregorian monks who maintained the church and hostel congregated in the tiny choir loft.

The pilgrims drifted toward the church and joined the four brothers for the evening service. The haunting cadence of Gregorian chanting echoed off the ancient walls and wafted over the weary pilgrims. Many sonorous voices, honed by years of communal singing, blended into one pure, trancelike monotone. All weariness and worry fell away. That night, a soft rain purred them to sleep. During the night, the temperature dropped, and drizzle turned to sleet, coating the path with an icy scrim.

In the morning brother Alfonso described the upcoming day's walk. "Today we will climb to the highest point of our journey. It is late in the season. We are lucky to cross now before fierce winter weather blocks the pass until spring. A short distance from the pass is the mountain of pebbles and the iron cross. As you know, it is a holy

125

place." Amika and Mateo nodded their heads. Brother Alfonso continued addressing his brothers. "Since before Christianity, the people have placed stones on the hilltop to mark the mountain pass. Romans deposited stones to honor their god Mercury. Thousands of pilgrims through the centuries have placed stones at the foot of the iron cross that the hermit saint, Gaucelmo, erected at the summit."

A bolt of recognition shot through Amika. *This is the place I was meant to reach! I have arrived.* Early the following morning the group followed Brother Alfonso to Ponferada, the town nearest the holy place. Each of the pilgrims withdrew into their own thoughts as they clambered up the hill. Soledad, Ignacio, and Esperanza waited at the base of the hill as Mateo and Amika scaled the icy slope.

Soledad tapped Amika's shoulder and drew her aside. "I cannot push the wheelbarrow up to the cross." She drew a plum-size rock from her pouch and placed it in Amika's palm. "Would you please take this rock and place it at the foot of the cross for us. It holds my prayers for Ignacio's miracle."

Amika ran her thumb over the smooth surface of the black stone. She met Soledad's misty eyes. Soledad, who had been as stoic as a Roman centurion, buried her face in Amika's shoulder and sobbed.

"Yes, of course. And I will add my own prayers for Ignacio's cure to yours."

Amika, Mateo, and the brothers joined the queue of pilgrims marching up the mountain of stones. At the summit she distanced herself from the others, withdrawing to a sunlit boulder. She sat facing the rising sun and pulled out her pouch. She withdrew the moon-faced stone, a symbol as old as the tribes who originally peopled the country at the foot of ancient mountains. She fingered the amulet Samuel had given her, depicting the tree of life and marveled that even a Jew so deeply respected this holy place that he would sacrifice something this fine. Soledad's glossy black stone lay in her palm beside the others. Finally, there were Father Jeshua's four amber stones.

The stones. Have I found the four lessons I was meant to learn from this journey?

The faces of those she had met along the way swam before her eyes. *Father Jeshua*—she remembered every detail of the dank cell from which he had saved her. *Without his mercy I would be a pile of ashes. Samuel the Jew—despite our differences in religion and status he was as generous as anyone I have known. Esperanza—such a small girl with such strength, willing to face withering danger with unflinching courage. She has taught me true bravery.* And there she stopped. Her mind went blank. No more visions, no more inspiration came to her. *My lessons are not complete. I have one more lesson to learn.* She returned one amber stone to her pouch. She stood and rejoined Mateo, resuming their trudge up the icy hill. At the summit she knelt at the foot of the iron cross and placed Ane's amulet, Soledad's black rock, the coin with an image of the tree of life, and three amber stones at its base. They lay with uncountable other mementos. Mateo watched her intently but kept his distance. When she turned to go, he rejoined her.

She felt hollow as she descended the hill. Distracted by her reverie, she ignored the slippery rocks beneath her feet. Her heel slipped off the edge of an icy rock and flew out from under her. Before she could catch her balance, she tumbled head over heels down the slope. She lay on her back, motionless. At first, she did not feel the pain. She lifted her weight to her elbows and looked toward her feet. Her lower leg angled grotesquely away from her knee. In the time it took for her heart to pound out two more beats, screaming pain replaced her numb detachment. Mateo scrambled down after her. He waved wildly at the brothers, who were making their own gingerly descent. "Help me! Help me! We need to get her down off this hill." Mateo stripped off his woolen cloak and rolled Amika on to it. "Each of you take a corner and we will bring her down."

127

They jostled and slid down the slope. The improvised litter bounced off rocks. With each bump Amika moaned, but they held tight to the cloak until they reached the bottom.

"There is a hospice at the Church of San Salvador in Ponferada near the base of the hill," Mateo said.

Amika had lost consciousness along with quantities of blood that seeped through Mateo's cloak, spattering the rocks below.

The hospital nestled on a sheltered ridge below the pass. When the sisters at the hospice saw a girl being brought to them on a makeshift litter, they hurried to the courtyard.

"This is bad. Bring her in. Quickly! Take her to the kitchen, not the dormitory. She will need more than a splint." Sister Immaculata assumed responsibility at once. She was heavy-set with smooth, ruddy skin and alert brown eyes. She spoke with decisive resolution, clearly used to being in control. Like a well-oiled machine they set to work.

"Sister Blanca and Sister Elena, hold her arms. Sister Carmen, hold her uninjured leg. Do not let her go. She will try to jerk away from you."

Sister Immaculata inspected Amika carefully. It was clear her condition was precarious. She dripped sweat; her skin was sickly gray; her heart pounded at twice its normal speed. The nun gently lifted Amika's eyelids. Her pupils were as big as a cat's at midnight. She crossed herself, rolled her eyes toward heaven then pushed and tugged the dislocated knee back into place. The pain jerked Amika back to consciousness. Her screams rattled the dishes on the shelves. With one more strong thrust, the nun forcibly yanked the lower leg into its correct position. Mercifully, Amika again lost consciousness.

"Sister Lucia, bring splints and bandages." Sister Immaculata issued orders with the efficiency of a well-seasoned ship's captain in a raging storm. "Find a bed for her. Bind both legs tightly to it. Then do the same with her arms. Make sure she cannot move."

She took an iron key from her belt. "Sister Carmen, go to my medicine cabinet and bring me the small brown glass bottle. I will give her ten drops of my most potent pain killer. No more than ten drops. It is an elixir of hemlock, henbane, and opium poppy. Any of those could kill her if we gave her too much, so watch what I do carefully."

Mateo, Esperanza, Soledad, and Ignacio, who had followed Amika's litter into the convent shuddered, hearing Amika's screams as they sat in the cloister's courtyard. Sister Immaculata returned to them, sleeves pushed up to her elbows, sweat beading on her forehead.

"We did our best. If fever does not claim her, she will recover, though I fear she will not have full use of her leg."

"Thank you, thank you. Can I speak to her?" Words gushed from Mateo.

"Maybe tomorrow. Tonight, you may sleep with the other pilgrims at our hospice. Sister Lucia, take these people to their cells."

Sister Lucia guided Mateo and the others down the dark hallway. Slate slabs laid horizontally without the benefit of mortar lined the corridor, absorbing the wavering light of Sister Lucia's candle. At the end of the hallway a dark-eyed nun pushed open a heavy door that led to a long, narrow room strewn with hay. Low partitions separated the pilgrim cells.

"These look like horse stalls," Ignacio said flatly.

"Yes, they certainly do. But we are fortunate to have found this place. Where would we be now if it weren't here?" Mateo looked around the room. "We could be on the side of that icy mountain with Amika. It is dry and safe here. Amika will be well cared for."

They awoke to a flawless blue sky. Though the September morning was cool, yesterday's ice was only a memory. After Sister Immaculata had tended to her injuries the night before, they had brought Amika to the hospital room where the four companions found her amid other injured pilgrims lying on narrow cots. Some had been less lucky with the bandits that haunted the path. Some contracted diseases from drinking bad water or eating moldy grain. Some were overcome by exhaustion and simply could not go on. Many suffered minor injuries from falls. Mateo clasped Amika's hand in both of his. His eyes searched her face earnestly. She was as pale as winter, her lips traced a thin chapped line across her face, her normally full, round cheeks were sunken.

"They say I can't leave this place for many weeks." Amika's face was a mask of desperation. Her voice was hoarse, and her words slurred. "By then it will be too late to go with you to Santiago. I have done what I came here to do. My mission is completed. But I had longed to continue walking with you."

"We will stay here with you," Mateo promised.

"No, you must finish your journey before winter sets in. You don't have much more time."

"How can I leave you like this?" Mateo clutched her hand between his and brought it to his mouth and gently kissing her knuckles.

Despite her pain she quivered in response to his touch. "The sisters will take care of me. You go. Unless you want to live in constant fear of arrest, you must prove to the bishop of Santiago that you've completed your penance and get your pardon." She gently pulled her hand away, wondering how they had gone from mere companions of the Camino to such tenderness. But there was no point in yearning for what she could not have. Mateo would be gone tomorrow. Who knew if she would see him again? If she did, it would certainly not be for many months.

"You were not meant to go Santiago, Amika. Your place is here. We will see you on our return journey," Esperanza said.

"Yes," Mateo brightened. "Winter will close the passes soon, but we will return next spring."

Mateo bent over and kissed Amika's forehead gently. Esperanza stood on tiptoes and kissed her cheek. Bright tears sprang to Amika's eyes. How long had it been since anyone had kissed her?

"We will see you again," she promised.

PART TWO

CHAPTER TWELVE
SANTIAGO

Santiago bustled with pilgrims who, like Mateo, Esperanza, Soledad, Ignacio, and the four brothers, had hurried to arrive before winter turned the pass into a no-man's land secreted under a thick blanket of snow. The holy city bustled with a carnival-like energy. Markets teemed with vendors hawking trinkets, cheap souvenirs, and relics. Musicians played lutes, bagpipes, psalteries, or flutes; their hats thrown to the pavement in front of them in hopes of gleaning a few coins from the pilgrims. Stands selling scallop shells, the symbol of St. James, sprouted on every corner and in every market. Scallop shells painted with the red cross of Saint James sprouted on pilgrims' packs all over the city.

The brothers were as confounded by the chaos as Mateo, Soledad, Ignacio, and Esperanza. Even Brother Alfonso, the only one of them who had been to Santiago before, was disquieted by the clamor.

"Follow me," he called to the others. He retreated to the shelter of a covered walkway. "Look at all these pilgrims wearing the cross of Saint James. Many of them have no respect for this holy place and are as profane as dancing bears. They have lost sight of the reason for the pilgrimage. I would not be doing my duty if I did not instruct my brothers, and you fellow pilgrims as well, of the real reason we come to this holy place." He paused, making sure that all eyes were upon him. "Do you know why we are here?"

"Yes," Soledad was certain of the purpose of her journey. "This is a place of miracles. St. James has the power to heal the sick if he chooses to."

"Yes, that is why people come here," Brother Alfonso agreed. "But there is a reason St. James chose this place and not another." He searched the faces before him.

"I know." Brother Juan bristled with impatience like a school boy waving his hand in the air to be called on.

"Please," Brother Alfonso extended his hand as if offering him a plate. "Tell the others." Brother Juan's eyes glistened as he launched into the story.

"Saint James was one of Jesus's apostles. After the crucifixion they all dispersed throughout the lands to spread the good news. Saint James made his way to Spain, seeking converts. But he was not successful. Only four people accepted the word of God. Discouraged, he returned to Rome, where Emperor Herod Agrippa beheaded him, along with two of his followers. After his martyrdom, a few of his fellow Roman Christians carried his body to the coast and put it into a stone boat with the bodies of the two disciples who died with him. The rudderless, unmanned boat, guided by angels, and carried by the wind and currents, landed on the western coast of Galicia where he had preached."

Juan pointed to the west where the land meets the sea.

"A wedding was taking place on the beach when his stone boat landed. It frightened the bridegroom's horse, which galloped into the surf. Both the horse and the bridegroom died. It was here Saint James performed his first miracle. He restored the bridegroom and horse to life, and they emerged from the water covered in scallop shells. The Queen of Galicia hauled the boat with the bodies of the saint and his two followers inland to this place, where the bodies laid forgotten for eight hundred years until Pelagius, a hermit, had a vision. In his prophetic dream he saw a field of stars. He followed the path of stars to an ancient tomb containing the bodies of Saint James and his followers. The hermit built a tiny chapel over the burial place. A small village named Campus de la Stella (Field of Stars) grew up there. News of the discovery spread like wildfire. At first, a trickle of pilgrims began to arrive, then a deluge. Ever since then, Saint James has performed miracles at this site. The tiny chapel grew into the

133

great Cathedral of Santiago where Saint James lies to this day, and where he still performs miracles."

"Thank you, Brother Juan. Well done." Brother Juan blushed until his face matched his red hair. "We must not allow the hawkers, performers, and insincere pilgrims distract us from the true meaning of the Camino de Santiago de Compostela," Brother Alfonso advised. "We will enter the cathedral together as we have walked together. Then I will take you to our monastery." He gestured to the laymen and women in the group. "You are welcome to stay at the hospice until you are settled in the city."

Mateo spoke up. "You are very gracious. We are sincerely grateful. Thank you."

Mateo, Esperanza, Ignacio and Soledad, and the brothers elbowed their way through the jostling crowd to the top of the cathedral's elegant staircase. Soledad held Esperanza's hand as if it were welded to her own. Mateo pushed Ignacio's wheelbarrow, making sure he would be safe in the roiling mob. They paused before the grand entry surrounded by other pilgrims. Prayers and hymns in many languages thrummed all around them. Some of the devout prostrated themselves at the doors. Others knelt for hours on the stones. Some slept like innocent children. nestled in their cloaks. Soledad hovered over Ignacio, endlessly repeating the rosary.

Even the magnificent Portico of Glory, as beautiful as it was, did not prepare them for the extravagance of the ornate interior. The apparent simplicity of the cross-shaped building was confounded by its huge proportions. Its ceiling soared more than sixty feet above them and the intricacy of its decoration staggered the imagination. Every surface was adorned with either masterful carvings or colorfully painted images.

A priest wrapped in lavish robes embroidered with gold and purple thread stood like an angel at the high altar and announced the indulgences being granted that day. For completing the pilgrimage one third of one's sins would be forgiven. For attending a mass celebrated by the bishop two hundred days in purgatory would be deducted from one's punishment in the afterlife. Stands sprouted in the side aisles, where prelates sold forgiveness to pilgrims desperate for absolution. Cripples hobbled in on crutches. The blind clung to the arms of their companions. Beggars crowded the three entrances to the cathedral. The poor mingled with the rich, seeking the intercession of Saint James.

Dozens of ornate chapels consecrated to different saints lined the interior walls. In each one a tray of small candles threw eerie shadows on the carved faces of the saints. Pilgrims dug through their pockets for one last penny with which to light a flame, hoping the saint would intercede for them.

"We are finally here." Tears streaked Soledad's face as she bent to embrace her son. She threw herself on the stairs before the high altar, pleading with God to reward her faith with a miracle. Ignacio tucked his limp legs under him, trying to kneel as best he could. Hot tears ran down his cheeks. He had not expected to feel such powerful emotions, but after walking hundreds of miles, here they were. The flames of hope evaporated his skepticism and he prayed as ardently as he ever had in his life.

After Soledad and Ignacio had settled themselves to pray, Mateo with Esperanza in tow, made a circuit around the opulent interior, marveling at the craftsmanship of the stone carvers. Though not as masterful as those of the Alhambra, they exuded an earnest yearning for the sublime. Early evening light angled through the splendid, stained-glass windows, casting multicolored flecks on the crowd. He returned to find Soledad and Ignacio where he had left them, bent over in prayer before the altar.

"It is getting late. We should go with my brothers to the monastery," Brother Alfonso beckoned them away.

"No, we will stay here," Soledad insisted. "We will stay here as long as it takes."

"Are you sure? Don't you want to eat? Please, come with me," Matteo offered. "You can return tomorrow."

"No, we will stay here. We did not come all this way to leave again after only a few hours."

Mateo knew neither he nor Brother Alfonso could dissuade her. "I understand. Esperanza and I will stay with the brothers at the monastery. We will bring you breakfast tomorrow."

He glanced down at the little girl, dwarfed by the scale of the monumental cathedral. A wave of unexpected emotion washed over him. He had grown to love this strange girl as if she were his own. She was an enigma. She seemed to hover between the ethereal and the prosaic. She had trekked such a great distance without complaint. They took her presence for granted and ceased being startled by her eerie premonitions. Mateo had never considered what would become of her when they reached their destination. Now, he thought perhaps she might have been better off staying with Amika under the watchful eyes of Sister Immaculata, but the girl had insisted on finishing the pilgrimage to Santiago.

The next day Mateo and Esperanza were back. They found Ignacio and Soledad exactly where they had left them. "You need a rest and a breath of fresh air. Please come with me. At least you can take a few minutes to walk around the plaza."

Again, Soledad refused. "Do you remember the miracle that came to the crippled man after thirteen days of praying? And do you remember Esperanza promising we would get our miracle here?"

Esperanza took Mateo's hand and drew him aside. "Let them stay for thirteen days. Then take them out to the plaza. This is what they need to do."

On the fourteenth day, Soledad again refused to leave the Cathedral. Both she and Ignacio looked haggard, with deep purple circles underscoring their haunted eyes, and skin as dry as fallen leaves.

"Today you will leave this place and your miracle will come to you," Mateo assured them.

Reluctantly Soledad wheeled a dejected Ignacio out a side entry and into the plaza. After so many days in the shadowy, cavernous cathedral they were blinded by the brilliant sun. Soledad's steps faltered and the barrow's wheel caught between two cobbles. The cart tipped to its side. Ignacio sprawled on the pavement. Soledad struggled to pull him upright, tugging at his armpits. Mateo hurried to Ignacio's side to lift him from the street.

Esperanza interrupted their efforts. "No, he will be all right. Leave him alone."

"I can't leave him floundering on the street like a wounded dove," Soledad objected. Mateo ignored the girl and moved quickly to rescue the awkwardly fumbling boy. Before he could lay a hand on Ignacio a stranger approached.

"Here, let me help you." A bedraggled old man stretched both arms toward Ignacio.

Mateo was startled by the man. He seemed to materialize out of nowhere. Grizzled hair stood out from his head as though it had not been combed for days. He wore a thick leather apron, blackened by soot. A dirty cloak hung around him, so stiff it could surely stand on its own. He had the hunched shoulders of a man perpetually bent over, and knobby, gnarled hands.

Ignoring Mateo's disparaging gaze, he explained to Ignacio. "I am an iron forger, a blacksmith. When my son was young, he was also crippled as you are. He suffered a terrible accident and could not walk. But I helped him walk again. If you allow me, I will help you as I helped him. Follow me."

Ignacio, Soledad, and Mateo exchanged astonished glances, as Esperanza smiled. They trouped after the bedraggled blacksmith who led them through the crowded streets, past the trinket vendors, food stalls, inns, and monasteries to a rough stone stall tucked into the city walls. Inside the soot- encrusted shop, a massive anvil stood before an inferno-like fire. Thin slats of iron hung from the rafters; mysterious looking tools lay about in disorderly piles.

"This is where I work. Come back tomorrow, and I will liberate this boy from crawling like a scorpion through his life."

"This is it!" Soledad cried when they were back in the street. "This is our miracle!" She knelt on one knee before Esperanza, squeezing the girl's small hands between her own. "How did you know? How did you know this would happen? Are you sent from God?"

"No!" Esperanza shrilled. "No! I am no miracle worker. I have told you before. My mother whispers to me. Why won't you believe me?" The smile had disappeared from her face, and she glowered beneath an angry, furrowed brow.

At the end of the day Mateo and Esperanza returned to the cathedral. Mateo walked a quick circuit around the nave, looking for a small chapel he had seen the day before dedicated to St. Giles, patron saint of cripples. He knelt before the statue and lit a candle. It hardly seemed enough to express his thanks for finding the blacksmith. He hung his head and thanked whatever powers had manifested this marvel.

The next day they wound their way through the narrow streets back to the blacksmith's shop. The grizzled man welcomed them warmly. He put aside the huge bellows he had been using to whip up a raging fire.

"Sit here, son." With some effort he lifted Ignacio onto a grimy table, so his legs dangled over the edge. Without a word of explanation, he took down one metal splint after another, holding them up against Ignacio's legs, calculating which would be the perfect size. He then wrapped a length of leather around Ignacio's ankles and shins to measure their circumference.

"Do you want to stay and watch me work?" he asked Ignacio. A brilliant smile transformed the blacksmith's face from that of a troll to a cherub.

"Yes, I would love to know how you work your magic, turning bits of metal into useful tools," said Ignacio. He thirsted for knowledge wherever he could find it.

The blacksmith looked at the others. Mateo and Esperanza nodded vigorously. Soledad's eyes were riveted on the blacksmith. She studied his every move.

"I could never leave, now that we are so close to our miracle."

He smiled at her sheepishly, abashed by the intensity of her attention, swelling with pride and purpose as he began to work. Sparks burst from the red-hot metal staves he pounded into the desired shapes. Every spray of sparks ignited a feeling in Soledad she had not felt in years. Sweat dripped from their faces and ran in rivulets down their backs as they watched metal being transformed into miracle. Their nostrils burned. An odor of iron dust and molten metal hung in the air. Yet no one said a word. He fashioned circular metal bands and welded them top and bottom to the staves. When he set them on the ground in front of the table, the braces stood by themselves. All that remained was to secure them around Ignacio's legs. He rummaged in a dark corner of the shop and found the old crutches his own son had used.

"Now, just do as I say." He gently slid Ignacio down until his feet rested on the ground. "Place the crutches firmly under your armpits and don't move them."

He bent down and carefully lifted one of Ignacio's knees then the other. "How does that feel?

"Heavy," Ignacio replied.

"That's right. The muscles in your legs have withered from disuse. You will need to practice every day. At first you must lean your weight against a wall or a table for balance. Then, supporting yourself on the crutches, lift each leg ten times. The next day lift them fifteen times. Keep increasing your repetitions until you can lift each leg fifty times. Only then may you stand away from the table and support yourself on the crutches.

"It will take patience and perseverance. But within six months you will be able to walk short distances. At least you will not need to be hauled around in a wheelbarrow, like a load of manure." He laughed. Tentative smiles bloomed on the pilgrims' faces.

Soledad was mesmerized by the contrast between his white smile and his soot-blackened face. She could not help noticing the strength in his sinewy hands and his muscular shoulders. Though bent by years at the forge, his muscles were still as strong and rippling as those of a bull bred for fighting in the arena. He was their miracle. She knew that. Ignacio's gait would be jolting and ungainly, but he would walk again.

"What is your name?" Soledad asked.

"I'm so sorry, I failed to introduce myself. My name is Salvatore.

Salvatore, savoir. Soledad's heart caught in her throat then swelled as if it would burst. She knew in her heart this feeling was more than appreciation. She cast her thoughts back to her youth. Ignacio's father had been a dissolute drunk, but at the beginning he had been funny, carefree, and charming. She was young then, and maybe it was only her youth that made her tingle in his presence, but she was taken in by him the same way a fish is pulled in by the fisherman's pole, inexorably, helplessly. She could no more swim away from him than that the fish could swim away from the hook. She did not know until much later, after Ignacio was born, how his weakness for drink would scar them all. Now, that long-forgotten tingling had returned as she looked at the blacksmith's radiant smile.

CHAPTER THIRTEEN

The following day, a thin drizzle coated the plaza in front of the cathedral of Santiago and the gray sky hung low and morose over the worshipers. Mateo rose early, leaving Esperanza at the monastery in the care of the cook's helper, who took a shine to the little girl. The day before, Mateo had scoured the shops for a comb and a bit of lye soap. He washed his threadbare clothes in the fountain in the cloister's courtyard as best he could, smoothing them with his scarred hands. He hoped his padded vest still conveyed an air of dignity. He drew himself up to his full height, steeled himself and strode to the bishop's palace, the Palazo de Xelmirez, adjoining the magnificent cathedral.

The sergeants at arms guarding the entrance eyed him grimly, their lances crossed, barring the entrance. "What business have you here?"

"This is my letter of introduction." Mateo reached into a pocket hidden in the lining of his vest and withdrew the document he had carried all this way from the magistrate in Jaen.

They ushered him in to a stone bench in the hushed entry hall. The bells tolled nine times, then ten, as he waited. He leaned forward, his forearms resting on his thighs, his head drooping over his hands clasped between his knees, as he stared at the Italian marble floor. When the guards returned, he jerked upright and stood abruptly.

"The bishop will see you tomorrow. Present yourself at ten bells."

The following morning, after a second washing of body and clothing, Mateo hoped he was even more presentable than the previous day. Confidence emanated from him as he approached the guards.

"I have an audience with the bishop. Here are my credentials." He withdrew the letter from the magistrate of Jaen again.

This time the guards stood aside, and the great oak doors swung open. An ornately attired page, a youth of about thirteen years, escorted him to the bishop's audience chamber in the great hall. Light streamed through the stained-glass rose window. Graceful arches resting on intricately carved corbels soared high above. Mateo ignored the grandeur of the chamber, hoping to give the impression he was unmoved by such luxurious surroundings. The bishop watched Mateo stride purposefully down the center of the long room, looking neither right nor left. *Good,* he thought, *this fellow looks like he is ready to get right down to business. He will not waste my time with pointless petitions.* He was right. Mateo went right to the heart of the matter that had brought him to this place.

"I have been unjustly accused," he began. "I have been punished for retrieving my own property from my own house in Jaen, after it had been confiscated from me."

"Is that right?" It was merely a rhetorical question Mateo was not meant to answer. The bishop extended his open palm. "Show me your documentation." The young page took the letter from Mateo and ferried it to the bishop's open hand.

"It says here that if you complete the entire journey from the Pyrenees to Santiago and present this document to me, you should be exonerated." He raised his eyes, taking the measure of the man before him. He could be considered handsome with his dark eyes and olive skin, but his demeanor exuded the wariness of a man whose experience had taught him that justice does not always prevail.

"Who did you bring as witness that you have walked the entire Camino?"

"Witness?"

"Yes, of course. Do you expect me to take you at your word without corroboration?"

Mateo rocked back on his heels. His eyes went vacant as he quickly assessed who might serve as witness. People come and go on the Camino. Their paths braid—meeting, separating, coming together again, eventually being replaced with new companions.

"I have not walked with any single companion all the way from the Pyrenees. I can bring a witness who will vouch for my walk from Burgos. Will that do?"

The Bishop fidgeted slightly, irritated that he had not already gotten rid of this man. "Bring this person back with you tomorrow." He was noncommittal. "I will make my judgment then."

For a third day Mateo presented himself to the bishop. This time he brought Soledad and Esperanza, who had attached herself to Soledad like a barnacle to a ship. It was nearly noon when they finally entered the reception hall.

Soledad held her head high, emulating Mateo's demeanor. She was suddenly acutely aware of her shabby appearance. She used all her self-control to focus on the prelate's narrow eyes and drooping jowls, and not on the magnificent room. She straightened and told her story. She added details—Mateo's bravery in dealing with the robbers, his gallantry in pushing her son's wheelbarrow, his stewardship of her crippled son and this motherless waif clinging to her hand. His guidance brought them safely to this place.

"None of these qualities are out of the ordinary along the Camino," the bishop replied. "Why do you think he will not steal again?"

The bishop hesitated. *What an unusual assortment of ragtag plebeians,* he thought.

Esperanza trained her large eyes on the bishop, studying his face.

"Search your heart," she said. "It will tell you this man is innocent. You know he has been selfless and brave in shepherding us to this place. Only good will come of pardoning him." Esperanza spoke in her compelling low voice, so unlike that of a child.

The bishop stared at the girl, dumfounded by her audacity. *She is right. No good can come of exacting more punishment from this man. He has friends among the powerful in Jaen. He has made his trek in good faith, and in good faith he must be exonerated.*

"Scribe!" he motioned to the monk standing behind his left shoulder dutifully making notes of the conversation. "Send this man away with the pardon he seeks. He has proven himself to be honest and charitable."

Mateo, Esperanza, and Soledad bowed and began to back out of the room. The bishop raised his right hand, palm facing the pilgrims.

"Our business here is not yet finished. There is a price for my mercy." Mateo's heart sank. "Master Mateo, you have the bearing and speech of an educated man. Do you have employment in Santiago?"

"No, your grace," Mateo hung his head. "I had not thought past the happy day when I would be free."

"Here is my judgment. You are clearly not an innocent man. Your hands bear the scars of a thief. I will grant you parole but not pardon. Not yet. Do you know Greek?"

"Yes, your grace," Mateo answered.

"And Latin?"

"Yes, of course. I also can figure sums. I have knowledge of geometry and philosophy."

"Good. I will grant your freedom after you have taught at the monastery school for two years." He flicked the back of his hand toward the pilgrims, dismissing them.

They backed out of the great hall with heads bowed, turning around only after they stood in the anteroom and the wooden doors had closed behind them.

"I'm free." Mateo heaved a sigh. He felt lighter and taller, as if a sack of rocks had been lifted from his shoulders.

Esperanza tugged his hand until he bent down to look at her. She stretched toward him and planted a chaste kiss on his cheek. Esperanza smiled enigmatically. Mateo reached down and wrapped his hands around the little girl's thin ribs. He lifted her high above his head and swung her around in circles, her legs flying out behind her. Esperanza squealed and laughed.

"We will go tell Ignacio. I assume he is with the blacksmith."

"Yes, he is," Soledad replied. "He is waiting for our return. He did not come because he did not want to divert the bishop's attention to himself. He will be overjoyed."

Ignacio barely looked up when Mateo, Esperanza, and Soledad ducked under the lintel into the sweltering shop.

"Salvatore is letting me help him," Ignacio said. He sat in a chair; his braced legs planted firmly on the floor. "He is teaching me how and when to pump the bellows, and how to judge the correct heat of the furnace." Ignacio's smudged face glowed with the joy.

"The boy is a natural. I wish my own son had taken such a keen interest in my work," Salvatore added.

Mateo, Soledad, and Esperanza watched in silence. Finally, Salvatore took the red-hot staves out of the fire with heavy tongs as long as a man's arm. He picked up a stone mallet as big as a melon and pounded the staves into a gentle curve.

He finally looked up. "Oh! I am so sorry. Where are my manners?" Steam billowed as he plunged the piece into a bath of water. "I was so involved at the forge I didn't ask if things went well with the bishop." Ignacio let the bellows rest in his lap.

"I am a free man. Or at least I will be after I serve my sentence. "The bishop granted me parole if I would teach for two years at the monastery school."

"I was called to bear witness to his worthiness by telling of his good deeds." Soledad beamed. "I spoke directly to the great bishop himself."

"Well, my boy, you can leave thinking about the terms of your parole for tomorrow, or next week, or next month." Salvatore clapped Mateo on the shoulder. "Today, we will celebrate with a drought of mead. It's my own concoction."

Salvatore banked the fire and invited them into the adjoining, two-room house he called home. Though modest and smoky, it was surprisingly well ordered. Salvatore's wares—repaired farm tools, cooking pots, and horseshoes, sat arrayed on a shelf awaiting their owners. A single ancient table of thick planks flanked by two benches took most of the space in one of the rooms. Iron pots hung from hooks affixed to a shelf holding his meager household goods, water basin and pitcher, a few pewter mugs, and an assortment of mis-matched crockery. A small window let in dim light. Salvatore lit the lantern. He pulled four pewter mugs down from the shelf, then dunked the dipper into a vat of mead standing in a corner.

"Here's to your freedom, Master Mateo." He lifted his mug smiling widely. "Your future awaits."

"Salud," Ignacio responded, delighted at being included in the adult merrymaking.

Salvatore seated himself next to Ignacio on the bench. He directed his attention to the boy whose elbows rested on the table. Ignacio was sitting normally for the first time in almost a year.

"Well, my boy, have you thought of what the future holds for you?" He draped his arm across Ignacio's shoulders like an old friend. Soledad smiled and joined them, taking a place at Salvatore's side on the bench, but said nothing.

"I didn't think I would ever walk. I avoided thinking about the future."

"You seemed to enjoy manning the bellows at the forge. Would you like to be my assistant?"

Ignacio straightened briefly but quickly slumped again like a boat loaded too heavy. "I doubt I could be much help," he mumbled. "Yes, today I could pump the bellows because I was sitting, but I cannot stand without the crutches. I will never be able to use my arms and hands properly as long as I depend on them." Ignacio threw off his dejection and smiled at Salvatore. "Please don't misunderstand. I am positively joyful at the prospect of moving under my own power. I will be grateful to you forever, but I'm afraid I'll never be a true apprentice."

"I disagree, my boy. With time and experience you can become quite agile with your crutches. I've helped others, and I can help you."

Ignacio looked into Salvatore's eyes, but did not respond.

"Tell me, Master Salvatore," Soledad intervened. "You mentioned a son who could not walk, like Ignacio." She looked away suddenly, her face reddening. "I am terribly sorry to bring back sad memories. I should not have asked. It was wrong of me to pry."

Salvatore ignored her apology. He stared into the distance and spoke quietly. "He was such a good boy, the center of my life after his sainted mother died giving birth to him. He would have made a wonderful partner. In the spring of his fifteenth year, he was called to the bishop's stables to shoe one of his horses, a high-strung Andalusian. A barn cat had given birth only a few weeks before and one of the mewling kittens rubbed against the horse's legs. The horse spooked and kicked my son in the back of the head. First, he lost the use of his legs, so I made him these crutches. Then he lost his sense of balance. Eventually he developed a palsy and could not control his movements. In the end he could not even swallow. He was taken from me one piece at a time, until in the end death came as a mercy." His shoulders sagged and his head drooped forward.

Ignacio placed a hand on Salvatore's gnarled fist. "I am here. If you think I could be useful, I will try to help you in any way I can. Though I may not become a skilled master like yourself, at least I can do errands for you, and pump the bellows."

"That would be a great comfort to me." Salvatore turned his misty eyes to Ignacio. Apart from his withered legs, the boy was strong and healthy, with bright, intelligent his eyes, and a refreshing youthful enthusiasm. For several moments he was quiet, considering the boy's proposition. He made his decision quickly and decisively. The chance of having a family again was irresistible.

147

"You and your mother can take my sleeping chamber. I will sleep in the shop. I have slept there many times. It will be no trouble."

"I will keep house for you. I can cook, clean, and help in the shop when you need me," Soledad offered. Then she shrank back, confused by her mixed emotions. "Of course, I would love to help," she said. "But I would worry about your reputation. Providing a bed and board for Ignacio as your assistant is perfectly acceptable. But what would people think of a live-in housemaid?"

"A housemaid?" Salvatore smiled. "I would never consider you a housemaid. My sensitivity to heat is high, but the heat I feel for you comes from within me." He grinned like a smitten schoolboy. "And if I'm not mistaken, you feel the same way."

"Are you proposing?" Soledad's eyes widened. "We have only just met!"

"Let's call it an apprenticeship." He winked at her. "If Ignacio proves as important to me as I know he will, we can be wed in the spring." His white teeth lit up his face. "By the time neighbors get around to wondering about us, we will already be wed."

This was a path forward for both herself and her son. She would not be alone anymore. Salvatore was indeed their miracle.

That evening Mateo and Esperanza returned to the monastery without their friends. After the silent evening meal, they sat side-by-side in the courtyard of the cloister. Mateo was lost in thought as Esperanza clung to his hand. A cool breeze hinted at the winter to come and reminded Mateo they would soon need to make living arrangements for the girl. Monasteries provided modest but decent living quarters for their nonreligious teachers. He would have a simple but comfortable room with bed, desk, and a kneeler facing an angular crucifix. More importantly he would have access to the scriptorium containing enough knowledge to satisfy his lust for learning.

Esperanza's small voice interrupted his reverie. "Yesterday, when you left me at the monastery with the cook's assistant, I saw classrooms where the monks were teaching local boys. Is there no school for girls?"

"A school for girls?" Mateo asked. He had never considered the possibility. Wealthy families either sent their sons to the monasteries to learn Latin, mathematics, logic, and rhetoric, or hired private tutors. Young men destined to inherit an estate needed these skills.

"Girls don't go to school," he said flatly. Esperanza's face drained of color, and she stared blankly into the distance. "There is no school for girls. But the nuns that run the convent take in orphans and charity cases and give them a rudimentary education. I will take you there tomorrow. It will be good for you."

Esperanza's eyes reddened and brimmed with tears. "I won't like it." Her lips parted like cracked clay.

Mateo contradicted her. "You don't know that. You may find a friend among the girls. Being around children will be good for you. Don't worry. You are a wonder, little friend." Mateo planted a kiss on the top of her head. "I will not abandon you. I will check on you."

CHAPTER FOURTEEN
PONFERRADA

Amika hobbled around the convent's kitchen. Her tunic had been replaced by a postulant's robes. She stooped down to the woodpile, picking out the driest tinder of just the right size to maintain an even temperature in the cavernous oven. The aroma of fresh-baked bread permeated the cave-like subterranean chamber. She pulled a large, flat paddle from the wall and slid it expertly under the golden loaves, gently depositing them on the massive stone table in the convent's underground kitchen.

Sister Carmen, head cook for the convent, had welcomed Amika's help. Preparing meals each day for twenty sisters was a never-ending chore. Despite her painful limp, Amika delighted in making herself useful. There was plenty to do. The sisters managed a flourishing farm, raising their own crops, caring for farm animals, threshing grain, splitting firewood. Self-sufficiency was a necessity for themselves and for the sick and poor to whom they ministered. When she was not in tending her crops, Sister Carmen lovingly looked after her beehives and vineyards.

During the previous winter when Amika's convalesced from her injuries, Sister Immaculata had taken time out of her schedule to sit with Amika, listening to her story. Like a miner searching for a hidden coal seam, she plumbed Amika's heart, searching for a spark of spiritual fervor she could nurture into the flame of a religious vocation. Despite the Mother Superior's time and attention, Amika remained a mystery. The girl was sincerely grateful for the kindness the sisters had shown her. She was guileless and honest, without a hint of deviousness. She was one of the most truly kind and generous people Sister Immaculata had ever met. Yet she remained aloof from the religious observances. Amika, when asked, did not even know if she had been baptized.

When spring unlocked the frozen rivers and freed the ice-imprisoned world, Amika retreated to the garden. In the buttery light of an early April morning Sister Carmen found Amika awkwardly sprawled in the rich loamy garden, her good leg tucked under her, the damaged one extended out to her side. With the expression of an ecstatic saint about to be lifted by angels into heaven Amika's eyes were closed. Her nose was buried in damp soil she held cupped in her hands

Sister Carmen coughed lightly, not wanting to startle her. "Would you like to help me with my garden this season?" She did not need to wait for an answer. Amika's face lit up like a daffodil on a dewy morning. She struggled to her feet.

"Thank you. It will be a joy and a pleasure." Amika's eyes glinted in the morning sun as a smile crept across her entire face.

Sister Carmen laughed. "In that case, we have some work to do. Do you have any carpentry skills?"

"Only if you call building rabbit traps carpentry," Amika responded.

"Well, we will learn together then."

Carmen and Amika pieced together scraps of wood to build garden beds raised about three feet off the ground, where Amika could work her magic without kneeling in the rocky soil.

As spring matured into summer Amika's vegetables and herbs grew profusely, their scents drawing the other sisters to the garden to marvel at the beauty of the beds.

"Show me what you have done here?" Sister Immaculata found the two young women with their hands buried to their wrists in the dirt, engrossed in transplanting an assortment of plants they had grown from seeds gleaned from last year's harvest. "I've been gardening all my life but have never seen such profusion. Where are the neat rows of carrots, and the tidy flower beds? Here, plants and flowers run amok with each other. I can't tell where the vegetable garden begins and the flower beds end."

151

Amika beamed. "Plants don't care about tidy rows. Like neighborhood friends, they favor some companions over others. These garlic plants thrive in the shade of the plum tree and associate with vines, like strawberries. They are also partial to carrots and potatoes. But do not like to be near beans and peas. Beans and peas have an affinity for marigolds and mustards. Alliums do best when planted near leafy companions like kale, spinach, chard, and celery. The squash thrives with nasturtiums." Amika's rattled on. "Sister - Carmen has a good knowledge of medicinal plants, so we grow those she finds useful, like yarrow to staunch nosebleeds. Some stimulate healing, or kill parasites, or reduce fever."

"God did not leave us helpless when he expelled Adam and Eve from Eden," Sister Carmen interjected. "We only need to learn where to find God's hidden treasures."

When summer faded into fall, Sister Immaculate took Amika aside. "You have been with us for a year now and have proven yourself eager and helpful. You and Sister Carmen have become fast friends. You wear the habit of a postulant of our community but have shown no devotion to a life of prayer. Though you attend Mass, you sleep through Matins and fidget during Sext. I cannot find the seed of a true religious vocation in your heart."

Amika twisted the edge of her habit into a hard lump.

"I have not pressed you on this issue. I wanted to give you time to adapt to our daily cycle of religious observance. The time has come for you to become a true bride of Christ or leave the community."

Amika's heart jumped, and her breath caught in her throat. Was she really being asked to leave? Amika knew Sister Immaculate was right, of course. She suffered through the daily round of prayers like an ox pulling a plow. It seemed a small price to pay for the secure life, the productive work, and the friendship of other women she now enjoyed.

"But Sister, where would I go? How would I support myself?" Amika choked on her words.

Unmoved, Mother Superior raised her chin and tucked her hands into her voluminous sleeves. "If you wish to serve God, dear girl, do it with the talents He has given you. You need not be a nun. Sister Lucia is a local girl and knows many people in town. Talk to her. She may help you find a suitable position. I know this comes as a shock to you. But it should not surprise you. Everyone here has taken their vows except you. You are healthy and your limp doesn't prevent you from working." Sister Immaculate hauled her bulky body upright and turned to leave. Amika stood deferentially as the Mother Superior departed, swaying like a boat in a gentle wind.

Amika retreated to her garden, and burrowing into the vines of the grape arbor, she tried to collect her thoughts. In the past year she had seldom left the convent, and then only when necessary and in the company of another sister. She knew almost nothing of the town. She understood that Ponferrada was a thriving village. But like any provincial town, it offered vanishingly slim prospects for a single woman. A woman could become a nanny, tending the children of the wealthy class. But Amika had no experience at all with children. She did not have friends when she was a child, much less brothers and sisters. The wealthy hired male tutors to educate their sons, but daughters learned whatever they needed to know at their mother's side. She could read and do sums at only a basic level. What was left to her? She could do menial labor, farm work, or the drudgery of a washer woman. But the local peasants were not prosperous enough to hire help outside their own families. Even if she could find work, where would she live? Insecurity and fear verging on panic gripped her.

The next day she sought out Sister Lucia, finding her in the common area spinning lamb's wool into yarn. "Sister, I need your counsel. Mother Superior has asked me to leave the community."

"Why would she ask you to leave?" Sister Lucia's placid stare was as calm as prayer itself. "You have been a great help to us." She paused, considered, and began again. "I understand," she said. "You have not taken your vows, and it is fairly clear you have no real wish to do so."

"Is it really that obvious?" Amika asked.

"I'm afraid so. Several of us have wondered when you would declare your intention to become one of us. When you did not do so after a full year, we expected you would soon leave us. I am not surprised Sister Immaculata made the decision for you." Sister Lucia's fawn eyes were full of sympathy. "How can I help you?"

"Mother Superior said you might be able to help me find a position in town, though I really can't imagine what I could do."

"Let me pray about this, and we will talk tomorrow. It wouldn't hurt if you also prayed for guidance." Her voice was kind but firm.

Amika knelt in her cell, pale moonglow bleeding in through a small window. She tried to recall the last time she had truly prayed, aside from sanctimonious words of the prescribed religious services. The voice of God spoke to her through the people she met, or through nature. She never sought, nor did she expect any personal connection with a Supreme Being. The Christian God was remote, ruling over every star in the universe, at the same time personally directing the lives of ordinary people as if they were marionettes. The Old Ways made more sense to her—gods and goddesses, spirits and sprites. She had a visceral connection to these beings. None were all-powerful. Each had a place in the natural and supernatural scheme of things. Amika knelt on her one good knee, the other extended stiffly behind her until exhaustion overtook her. Morning found her curled up on the cold stone floor. In her heart she knew Sister Immaculata was right. As much as she loved her life in the convent, she did not belong here. After morning prayers, Amika again sought out Sister Lucia.

"Good morning, Amika." Lucia eyes twinkled happily. "I have thought of something that might suit you very nicely."

"How kind of you." Amika was genuinely delighted.

"I have a friend who offers simple foods to pilgrims on their trek to Santiago. She asks for donations but does not deny food to anyone. She earns enough to support herself. She is a widow and lives alone. She might have some advice for you. Her name is Gabriela. Her home is easy to find. It is in the center of town, right on the path of the Camino."

"Thank you, Sister Lucia. I will talk to her today."

Amika had no trouble finding Gabriela's house. Like the other buildings in the center of town, hers was a narrow, two-story stone building sharing walls with its neighbors. The ancient buildings had settled together over the centuries and leaned against each other in crooked camaraderie, like drunken old men. Two window openings on each story canted to the left, and the was door no longer square. Light leaked through the gaps between the cracked door and its warped frame.

Gabriela stood behind a sturdy table, her stained apron covering a simple peasant dress. An undecorated ceramic bowl filled with steaming bone broth stood next to several round loaves of bread. A small bunch of radishes, a few bittersweet late summer apples, and deep purple plums rounded out her offerings.

She smiled broadly as Amika approached her table. "You are my first customer today, please let me offer you an apple free of charge."

Amika smiled and accepted Gabriel's offer. "I am her to see you," she said. "Sister Lucia suggested I talk to you."

"See me? I can't imagine why."

"I was walking the Camino," Amika began. "But a serious injury ended my journey. I have been living at the convent since last autumn. The nuns nursed me back to health. I was hoping I could help you."

Gabriela's smile faded. She scrutinized the young woman before her. She had a round, honest face, and large expressive eyes. Not beautiful, but appealing. "I don't need help. I am sorry. I barely survive myself and certainly can't support another."

"I was hoping I could help you," Amika repeated. "I have ideas for increasing your business. I promise I will earn my keep." Amika liked Gabriela already. She was straight-forward and candid. She was in her middle years, older than Amika but not eroded by time. Her hands were delicate with long fingers, but it was clear they were no strangers to hard work. She wore a head cover like Basque peasant women of her home country. Her figure was well rounded, like a peasant farmer's wife. Her deep-set, bright blue eyes sparkled beneath a high forehead.

"And you said Sister Lucia sent you? She is my cousin, you know. Our mothers were sisters. She is a peaceful soul. No one was surprised when she took holy orders."

"Yes, she is kind and thoughtful. She is happy in her vocation." Amika stopped to let Gabriela remember her cloistered cousin. "I think I can help increase your business," Amika forged on. "I have a thorough knowledge of plants."

"I have my own kitchen garden. I don't need more plants."

"Would your customers be interested in medicinals? I can grow healing herbs and can also hunt wild plants that cure all kinds of illnesses. My mother was a healer. I learned at her knee."

Gabriela folded her arms across her generous bosom, considering her response. She was in no hurry. Amika returned her gaze. She stood calmly before Gabriela, arms at her sides, striving to appear neither anxious nor brash.

"I will consider your proposal. Bring me a sampling of the specimens you think would be of interest to pilgrims and townspeople. Take your time. There is no hurry."

"Thank you," Amika gave Gabriela a quick nod. "I look forward to seeing you again soon."

Later that day Amika limped to the edge of town and looked up the slope to where the fields ended, and the wild things grew. It would be a challenge. Leaning heavily on her walking stick she took first one step, then the next. She knew what to look for. Yarrow was easy enough to find, as it grows in almost any sunny meadow, as did potentilla and mustard. In the shrubby margins between open field and dark forest she found sage. Before returning to her convent cell, where she would bundle and hang the plants to dry, she passed by a miller's pond, and found some asparagus and duckweed. That would be enough for now. She knew there would be many more useful wild plants waiting for her when spring returned next year. That night her knee swelled and throbbed. She was no stranger to pain, but she knew she would need to take extra care of her knee if she expected to be useful to Gabriela.

When her plants had dried, Amika returned to Gabriela's house. She watched as Gabriela cheerfully greeted each pilgrim and doled out her simple offerings, bread, bone broth and root vegetables. *I could help Gabriel. We could offer remedies to alleviate the maladies common among the weary, footsore travelers.* With that in mind, Amika raised a hand in greeting and offered her best smile.

"I have some ideas to share. Tell me what you think."

One by one Amika presented her plants. She laid a bundle of yarrow on the table. "I'm sure you recognize yarrow. It grows everywhere. It will help anyone with wounds, especially those that are not healing well. And this potentilla reduces fevers. Mustard relieves inflammations of the throat and stomach and fights rheumatism. Pilgrims will appreciate these remedies." Amika warmed with enthusiasm as she spoke. "There are so many other wild plants that can cure illness, relieve pain, heal internal maladies, and soothe the ailments common among pilgrims. I was a pilgrim myself until I injured my knee." Amika listed to the side like an old fence post, supporting her weight on her undamaged leg.

Gabriela's demeanor remained stiff, and she paid no attention to the bundled plants Amika laid before her. "I noticed that you walk with a pronounced limp." Gabriela observed. "Don't you have a poultice or salve to relieve the pain?" hinting that a purported healer should be able to heal herself.

157

"There are herbs that help pain, but many of them are also dangerous, like belladonna," Amika mumbled. "and many are not available in autumn. I am using only the simplest remedies. But the damage to my knee cannot be cured. I am fortunate that the good sisters were able to restore my ability to walk."

"I have something that will help strengthen that knee." Gabriela held out a shallow bowl. "Please, have some of my bone broth. It is the best thing for bad joints." She watched as Amika's wide eyes peeked over the rim of the bowl as she drank the broth.

"This is delicious bone broth. What did you put in it to give is such flavor?"

"I have added squeezed lemon, a bit of sea salt, and a touch of oregano." Gabriela beamed with pride. Amika's enthusiasm invigorated Gabriela as a cool breeze enlivens the weary at the end of a hot summer. Neither of them spoke for many minutes. Gabriela tried to imagine the two of them tending to the needs of pilgrims, Gabriela to their hunger, Amika to their health. *It would be nice to have a partner,* she thought. *I have been so lonely since my husband died.*

"Yes, I think we will be good for each other," she admitted.

* * *

Winter winds howled down from the pass and swirled through the streets, assailing those few souls who ventured out. But the walls of Gabriela's narrow house were unimpressed. They had already withstood over a hundred merciless winters. Protected inside the shelter of old stones, Amika and Gabriela huddled together in front of a lively fire in the hearth, heads bent together over a charcoal drawing of next year's garden. Though the patch of ground behind the house was small, they carefully plotted the most efficient use of the space. When spring broke winter's grip, they would be prepared to offer an assortment of tasty vegetables and simple remedies. In four short months, spring would arrive, and they would be ready.

CHAPTER FIFTEEN
SANTIAGO
1254 AD

"Mother Superior says you have learned much in the convent school."

Mateo and Esperanza sat in shade of the well-tended courtyard surrounding the cloister as they had almost every month for two years. The hours of sunlight were noticeably shorter, as summer begrudgingly gave way to autumn.

"I have," Esperanza said bluntly. "I've learned to scrub floors, clean ashes from the hearth, scour pots, and take orders from the cook. They tell me they are providing me training, so I will be prepared for a position in a good household until a man finds me. Then I will be his scullery maid instead of theirs."

Mateo lifted her face upward toward him. She was no longer a little girl. She was all spindly arms and legs. And though her face had lengthened, her deep-set thunderstorm eyes glared as intensely as ever.

"Yes, Esperanza. All that you say is true, but you have also learned to read and do sums, haven't you? Those skills should give you some comfort."

"I have, but all I am allowed to read is the bible and the missal of prayers."

"I understand, really I do. You are restless and no longer want to be confined in this place. You are older now. Your mind has stretched as much as your arms and legs."

Esperanza's eyes drilled into Mateo. Without looking at her he could feel their heat. "You are restless too," she declared.

"You are right, of course. It is impossible to hide anything from you. I have served my 'parole.' I have taught at the monastery for two years. For the first time since I fled Jaen, I am truly a free man. I have earned some money. I am healthy and strong. Yet, I am yearning for something more."

"I know what you are looking for." Her eyes slid sideways toward him and the hint of a smile toyed at the corners of her mouth. "I miss her too."

Mateo turned his head sharply toward Esperanza and sucked in a hot breath.

"You don't even realize it yet, but she is where your future is." She sounded like Mateo imagined the oracle at Delphi would have sounded, her voice unnaturally deep and sonorous.

Mateo had not heard Esperanza's low, alien voice for the two years since they'd arrived. He had assumed that she had outgrown her uncanny intuition, but there it was, pointing out the truth as accurately as a sundial marks the hours of the day. Silence descended and time ground to a halt. The birds alone, clustered around the fountain, drinking, bathing, and darting into the branches of the courtyard's single apple tree, broke the stillness.

"You know it is true, don't you?" Esperanza picked up the broken threads of the conversation.

"I see her face at night when I should be sleeping. I wonder every day if she has recovered from her injuries, if she ever left the convent, if she is happy ..." Mateo trailed off.

"You know we can walk back as easily as we walked here."

"Well," Mateo gave his head a definitive shake and raked his fingers through his black locks. "If we leave now, we can return to Ponferrada before winter sets in." He stood, took Esperanza's hand, and walked her back to her cell. "I will go have a talk with Mother Superior."

* * *

The days of looking like tattered peasants were behind them. They outfitted themselves with well made, practical clothing of the best materials. Mateo wore a sturdy woolen cloak, over a cotton tunic rimmed at the edges with intricate embroidery. He had purchased a few decorative adornments to indulge his vanity. A fine bronze brooch fastened his cloak at the throat, and a thick, hand-tooled leather girdle belted his cotton tunic. He wore leather boots over wool leggings. A felt hood covered both head and shoulders, and a wide-brimmed straw hat was tied under his chin like a bonnet to protect him from the sun.

Esperanza, on the other hand, looked like a miniature lady with a stiff wimple framing her face. Her hair was covered by a veil of sumptuous blue linen. made specially for her by Sister Bernadette, the seamstress, who could not resist the elegant touch blue linen imparted. Even the businesslike Mother Superior surprised her with a corded belt from which a fine silver crucifix swayed, knocking against her knees as she walked.

The sun had swung to the north like a hinged door, heralding the change of season. Mateo and Esperanza meant to complete their journey before it slammed shut and cold weather returned.

They walked east for two weeks against a tide of pilgrims flowing toward Santiago. With new eyes they noticed their haggard faces, their bandaged feet, their stained, threadbare clothing. Despite the rigors of the pilgrimage, most of them exuded hope, knowing their journey was almost over. Each of them carried the burden of their own sins, their own stories, their own dreams.

"It feels like I'm walking through mud. Fragments of their various stories cling to me like clots of clay as the pilgrims pass me. Even if they are silent, I can feel them." Esperanza confided.

"For me it feels like walking backward in time," Mateo said as he unconsciously massaged his scarred hands. When I walked this way as a pilgrim, I was a branded thief. I was nearly penniless, a battered wreck of a man wallowing in the injustice of my fate."

"We are not walking into the past. There is a future waiting for us," Esperanza reminded him.

Mateo ached to ask the girl what she saw in their future. Would it be happy, he wondered? Why would he leave an honorable position teaching at the monastery school just to follow an ineffable longing that clouded his heart like fog. It was understandable that Esperanza would want to leave the convent life she detested and return to a friend who was as close to a mother as she would ever know.

"Calm your heart, my dear Mateo," she said. "Your questions will be answered soon." She smiled up at him, reading his disconcerted look. "It doesn't take a mind reader to understand your longing. It is written on your face—in the creases growing into permanent furrows between your brows, the sagging lips, and the rounded shoulders. She will think you're an old man." Esperanza giggled, and for a moment she became just a lanky girl longing for joy.

The road grew steep as they retraced their steps through Galicia. Slate tile roofs slick with mist protected simple stone houses that dotted the trail like rosary beads. The valleys sheltered tiny villages; mere collections of simple stone houses clustered around ancient stone churches devoid of decoration. Stone fences, the painstaking work of generations of peasants, divided the fields into plots barely large enough to support a family. Ox carts rumbled by. Hunched women in tattered shawls and dark clothing slogged through muddy yards tending meager gardens.

Bridges constructed to facilitate pilgrims' passage arched gracefully across river crossings. Templars guarded bustling towns built on the bones of Roman encampments. Market towns along the way bustled with people trading the last of the season's crops for spindles, whetstones, fat capons, eggs, butter, and cheese. They backtracked through fields of ripened wheat and flax. Olives, grapes, and fruit, waiting for harvest drooped from every branch. Ruined ancient castles and the hulking walls of more recent fortresses glowered down at them from hilltops.

Mateo had amassed a bit of money teaching at the monastery school. In his pouch he carried the maravedi Samuel the Jew had given him. His coins bought them the luxuries of private hospices, and ample food. On one rainy day, they even purchased a ride on farmer's cart, sparing them from a muddy slog over rough terrain. All the while they gained elevation, and as they did, they lost the warmth of the sun. By the time they reached Ponferrada, almost two weeks later, they realized they would not be able to return to Santiago until the following spring.

CHAPTER SIXTEEN
PONFERRADA

When Mateo and Esperanza arrived in Ponferrada, the flood of pilgrims on their way to Santiago had dwindled to a trickle. Merchants hawked their wares, noisily enticing the stragglers with end-of-season bargains. They retraced their way back to the convent. Their excitement and apprehension grew with every step. Mateo lifted the iron door knocker and pounded it soundly against the heavy door. They could hear the sound reverberate inside. Sister Lucia opened the door and stared blankly at the pair of visitors.

"How can I help you?" She scrutinized them closely, puzzled by their familiarity. "Do I know you? Have I seen you before?" she asked, glancing back and forth from man to child.

"Yes, two years ago four Benedictine brothers brought an injured young woman, a friend of ours, to your door. We have returned to inquire about her recovery."

"Oh yes, now I remember. You are talking about Amika. She no longer lives with us, but you can find her in town. She stays with my cousin, Gabriela. They sell food and herbal medicines to pilgrims from a stand in front of Gabriela's house. Just follow the Camino through town and you will find her."

Mateo and Esperanza found the two women standing behind a table arrayed with simple pilgrim fare. Mateo and Esperanza stood in the shadows of a recessed doorway watching the women carrying on their business from behind a stout oak table. A plump older woman, with gray hairs mixed with the brown escaping from her headscarf, offered a few small, white potatoes balanced on her extended palm toward a scrawny pilgrim.

A kind smile lit the round face of the younger woman. She held a small bunch of dried thyme up by its bundled stems, showing it to a woman holding the hand a young girl with a bad cough. The younger woman limped noticeably as she disappeared into the house and emerged with a cup of hot water. She wrapped the bundle of thyme in a porous cheesecloth and dipped it into the steaming cup, chatting amiably with the mother as they waited for the tea to steep. She then bent down and patted the girl's fevered cheek. The girl sipped the tea as her mother dropped a coin into Amika's hand. Amika and her customer exchanged nods and smiles, then the woman and girl turned and walked away down the street.

When afternoon shadows lengthened and Amika and her partner began gathering up their wares, Mateo and Esperanza approached the table. Amika froze, standing bolt upright as she watched the two figures emerge from the recessed doorway. Her heart battered her ribs. She forgot to breathe. The blood drained from her face.

"What is it?" Gabriela supported Amika's bent elbow to prevent her from toppling over. Amika did not say a word. Gabriela followed Amika's eyes and saw a man and a girl approaching. "Who are they?"

Again, there was no answer.

"We are just closing up here, as you can see. Is there something I can help you with?" Gabriela asked the pair.

"Amika, we returned to find you," Mateo said, ignoring the questioner.

"Yes, our hearts had an empty space where you should have been," the girl spoke. "We missed you, so we came back to you."

Amika was transfixed, not moving, or speaking.

"Who are you? What do you want with my friend?" Gabriela moved out from behind the table and stood protectively between the visitors and Amika, her fists planted firmly on her hips.

The spell Amika was under broke and she regained use of her tongue. "It's all right, Gabriela. These two are my friends. They walked the Camino with me. For me, the journey ended, but they traveled on to Santiago. Let me introduce you."

"Well, it sounds like you have some catching up to do. Amika, you may invite them inside and they can explain their sudden appearance." Gabriela gestured for them to follow her into the house.

That night Gabriela realized Amika had shared only a corner of the complex tapestry that wove the lives of these three people together. Mateo recounted his odyssey from Jaen to Santiago for their hostess, and Esperanza told of her heartbreaking journey from abandoned orphan to rescued child, then to her confinement at the convent in Santiago.

"Did you get your pardon from the bishop?" Amika asked Mateo.

"Yes, I did, but he also imposed a penalty of two years parole, which I spent teaching at the monastery school. It was not an onerous task. I found I enjoyed teaching. That is the reason we did not return sooner."

"But we missed you!" Esperanza interrupted. "We both had a hole in our hearts, as I said. I knew we needed to come back to this place to truly complete our journey."

"Hmph," Gabriela huffed at the dramatic tales. "And what will you do now? I cannot take you in. Amika and I are living in each other's laps as it is. I never intended to give her room and board. But the Mother Superior threw her out. What else was I to do?"

Amika's face reddened. "I didn't intend to impose on you, Gabriela. You have been so generous with me. I could only repay you by finding a way to help. I'm sure my friends had no intention of asking you for a place to stay."

"Don't feel bad, dear girl. You have been a great blessing to me. I do not regret taking you in." Turning to Mateo, Gabriela continued. "Did you know Amika has a thorough knowledge of gardening and herbal medicine?" Gabriela asked with evident pride.

"Yes, we have some idea of her talents. She found food for us when we were robbed. But that's another story." Mateo stood, smoothed his embroidered tunic, and took Esperanza's hand. "It's getting late. We will return to the convent's hospice tonight, and tomorrow we will begin puzzling out our future here."

Amika crouched to embrace Esperanza. "I hope you understand. You know I would take you in if I could. But this is not my house and Gabriela is correct. The space here is very limited."

Esperanza stared blankly at Amika. This was an outcome she had not foreseen. She managed a wan smile. "Our futures were bound together from the night my mother sent you to me. We will find our way together. Soon we will be a family."

Amika stood and extended her hand to Mateo. He leaned forward, his lips grazing her knuckles as if she were a fine lady. A jolt like lightning shot through her, standing the fine hairs on her arms on end. Amika stared resolutely at the ground, hiding a storm of emotions engulfing her as Mateo and Esperanza turned and walked back toward their familiar convent cells.

The next morning Mateo entrusted Esperanza to the care of the corpulent cook who was happy to set the child to work. Esperanza pulled a glum face, but Mateo was having none of it. "Amika was right, you know. She is not in any position to impose on Gabriela. And you saw the house. It is even smaller than the blacksmith's house. She is lucky to have a patch of ground large enough to grow a few vegetables. What would you have her do? Let you sleep under the dining table?" Esperanza did not answer. "You said yourself that our futures are entwined. Now is the time to trust your intuition. In fact, you can ask your mother's spirit to help us find a house." He winked.

"Don't mock me!" Esperanza shrilled as she stomped.

Mateo smiled. *Good, he thought. I'm getting a reaction from her. Anger can be a useful emotion. It serves her better than resentment.*

He set to work scouring the town for lodgings for himself and Esperanza. In a narrow street two lanes away from Gabriela's house, Mateo found a vacant building. His prosperous appearance gained him the cooperation of a neighbor, who directed him to the home of the property's landlord in a prosperous neighborhood several blocks away.

The landlord's house proudly took its place among other elegant buildings on the street. Mateo knocked on the door and waited, his hands crossed in front of him as he surveyed the building. Its stalwart exterior walls were of rounded river rock with decorative squares of smooth stone at the corners. A shallow wrought-iron balcony, barely deep enough for potted flowers, protruded from the second story. On the balcony, a double door stood open to the street below. Mateo knocked a second time. Finally, a uniformed servant opened the door. After Mateo explained his purpose, the servant led him to the landlord's cluttered office. Before the bells tolled the Sext, the noon hour prayer, their business was completed. The landlord handed Mateo a heavy key ring. Mateo had paid almost all his remaining gold coins to lease the empty building for a period of two years.

His buoyant strides brought him back to the convent where he collected Esperanza, now happily coated in flour. "Take the apron off, dear girl, let's go find Amika and Gabriela."

The two women stood at the table before Gabriela's door with their vegetables and dried herbs. The bowl with pilgrims' donations was almost empty. It was not going to be a prosperous day for them.

Mateo practically bounded up to their stand.

"Come with me," he ordered. "Put your things inside, close the door and come with me." He grabbed Amika's hand and pulled her along. "You come too, Gabriela. This surprise is for both of you."

The foursome trundled down the street until they stood in front of the vacant building.

"Here it is," Mateo began. "It is ours for two years. We must make the most of it." He stood tall and pulled the keys to the ornate lock from his cloak.

They wandered the first floor together. As the shock wore off, the opportunities the building offered dawned on them like a warm summer sun. The rooms were simple but spacious. There was a central great room with a hearth large enough for a person to stand upright. The front of the fireplace opened to the living area and the back side to the spacious kitchen behind it. A loft supported by heavy timbers protruded, overhanging the great hall below.

"This room is large enough for storage," Mateo said pointing to the loft. "And I can sleep there as well. Follow me."

He practically dragged them to the rear entry door. A walled garden, overrun with weeds and vines, lay open to a patch of sky above.

"A garden!" he crowed.

Amika and Gabriela embraced and pounded each other's backs.

"We will be able to make a home for Esperanza. She can help us in the garden," Gabriela chimed in.

"We will set up a spacious table with the best seasonal foods, hearth-hot bread and balms for every ailment," Amika rhapsodized. "Esperanza has the intuition of a seer. She will know exactly what ailing pilgrims need to soothe their aches and injuries."

"I will find a position at the monastery school," Mateo said with less enthusiasm. "I have a dream of teaching my own private students. If we save our money, I will be able to set up a small school here. No monastery, no strictures imposed by others. I will be able to teach the full range of classical knowledge as I was taught." His eyes glowed. Amika had never seen him so passionate about anything.

Gabriela's narrow house looked even smaller and shabbier when they returned that evening.

"I will tell the landlord that we are moving out," Gabriella said with her customary bluntness. "My husband found this place for us when we were both young. When the coughing disease took his life, the landlord was kind enough to allow me to stay, charging me rent far below what he could demand from a new tenant. He will be happy to get its full value by finding a new tenant."

CHAPTER SEVENTEEN
SPRING 1255

The banked embers of the kitchen fire cast an orange glow over the great room. Amika prodded the fire to life and gingerly laid on two small pieces of firewood, then sat on a bench leaning her back against the trestle table. For yet another night, disturbing dreams had woken her. They were always the same. She was back in the Basque village of her childhood, wandering the murky mountain trails, searching, searching, but not knowing what she was meant to find. She had the vague impression that she was looking for a person, someone she knew but could not name. He was close by. She could feel his presence, but she could not see him.

The first winter in their comfortable new home had been mercifully mild, but their depleted stores forced them to rely on a hermit-like diet of dried lentils and freeze-softened potatoes. Mateo trudged through slushy streets to the Monastery school to teach the gentry's spoiled sons. He gleaned uneaten scraps from the monastery kitchen and brought them home to Amika, Esperanza, and Gabriela.

Spring arrived. Gone were the slushy mounds of dirty melting snow that had turned the streets into a quagmire. The plans Amika and Gabriela had laid out for the garden over the winter were now on the cusp of coming to fruition. Amika rejoiced over their carefully planned beds of vegetables, fruit, herbs, and flowers. Sage, hyssop, comfrey, calendula, storksbill, and yarrow grew in charming geometric patterns next to beans, cabbage, carrots, leeks, and radishes.

An early cold snap propelled the two women into the garden with scraps of cloth to cover the tender spring shoots. Amika was chilly as she dozed off before the fire, her blanket around her shoulders. Her dream returned, but this time rather than wandering through the wooded trails, she searched the city streets. She turned a corner and there he was. She came face to face with the object of her longing. It was Mateo. Her heart rattled in her chest, heat suffused her body, a powerful magnetism drew them toward each other. Their embrace was an ardent, burning, urgent need. Amika jolted awake, aroused by the intensity of her dream.

"You were dreaming." Mateo had materialized beside her on the bench before the fire, his voice as soft and dark as black velvet.

"I need you," Amika whispered. "I need you like the tender shoots need spring rain. I ache with longing."

"I know," Mateo wrapped her in his arms. "I have resisted climbing down from my loft and finding you in the night. I burn as you do. I could feel your desire."

Amika enveloped him in her blanket. Their union was at once as fiery as a forge and as soothing as a cool lake. It was the last time they felt alone. Before first light Amika crept back to her bed. Esperanza stirred and mumbled in the husky voice of dreams. "It has finally happened. This is how it was meant to be."

SUMMER 1255

Saffron fingers of light caressed the rocky slope up to the Cruz de Ferro. Amika crept out of the house as soundlessly as a stalking cat. By the time the town was fully awake she would have returned to her kitchen, preparing for the raucous boys who would take over the great room. Mateo would be welcoming them to his new Classical Academy of Ponferada.

She leaned heavily on her walking stick, praying she would not slip as she struggled up the pebbly slope. Soon the hilltop would be thronged with pilgrims of all sorts, depositing tokens of their hopes, prayers, and penitence at the foot of the cross. At this early hour, however, Amika had the hill to herself. At the top she reached into her pouch and withdrew the last of the four stones Father Jeshua had given her.

Was it only three years ago? Surely not. *It has been a whole lifetime*, she thought. She knelt painfully on one knee as she reverently placed the last stone at the foot of the cross. The voices of the past echoed in her head. *Father Jeshua taught me mercy. Samuel the Jew taught me generosity. Esperanza taught me bravery. Mateo has taught me love, the final lesson. I have found my way.*

---

[i] adapted from The Miracles of St James, Thomas Coffee, Maryjane Dunn, 2009, Italica Press

Made in the USA
Monee, IL
27 March 2022

93635376R00111